The Eye of the Heart

The Eye of the Heart

An Introduction to Sufism and the Major Tariqats of Anatolia and the Balkans

By
Yaşar Nuri Öztürk

Translated by
Richard Blakney

Redhouse Press
Istanbul

ISBN 975-413-024-8

THE EYE OF THE HEART

Copyright 1988 Redhouse Press
Cover Photo: An oil painting by F. Zanaro,
                    from the archives of Taha Toros.
Photos in text: Illustrations 1-9, 11-12, 14-38,
                    and 40-46 by Haluk Konyalı;
                    10, 13, 39 by Redhouse Press.
Typeset by: İstanbul Matbaası
Printed by: Boğaz Ofset

REDHOUSE PRESS
Rızapaşa Yokuşu No: 50
Mercan 34450 Istanbul
Tel: 522 14 98—527 81 00

Translator's Note

The English text of this book is the product of the translation, condensation, and simplification of a much longer Turkish text prepared by Dr. Öztürk for the Redhouse Press. The condensation and simplification were undertaken jointly by Dr. Öztürk and myself in order to make the essence of a highly technical text available to a wide readership.

Instead of attempting to translate Dr. Öztürk's Turkish renderings of Koranic verses, I have quoted the English renderings done by M. M. Pickthall in his *The Meaning of the Glorious Koran*. In those instances in which a word or phrase of Dr. Öztürk's Turkish rendering differed substantially from Pickthall's English rendering, I have altered Pickthall's translation to make it conform to the interpretation given by Dr. Öztürk. All translations of poetry appearing in the text are my own. In translating the poems by Yunus Emre I relied heavily on the interpretations given by Murat Sertoğlu in his *Yunus Emre Divanı ve Açıklamaları*.

Special thanks are due to Mrs. Sema Kırsalı who patiently proofread and typed the various revisions of the English text for this book.

Richard Blakney

Acknowledgements

Acknowledgement is due to the following for plates in this book: Topkapı Palace Museum Library, Istanbul, 1-9, 11-12, 14-38, 40-46; Diwan Literature Museum, Istanbul, 10, 13, 39. Thanks are due to the Directorates of both these museums, and especially to Dr. Filiz Çağman,Curator of the Topkapı Palace Museum Library.

Preface

This book is an introduction to sufism, the sufism of the *tariqats* (dervish fraternities) in particular. From among the great number of *tariqats* which have existed in the Islamic world I have selected for consideration only those which had large numbers of followers among the Turks of the Ottoman Empire. This decision was largely determined by the fact that these particular *tariqats* are the ones with which I am most familiar, their having been for many years one of my subjects of study.

The first part of the book is an outline of the principles and history of sufism. It begins with a discussion of how sufism is related to the Koran and the *sunnat* of the Prophet Muhammad. This is followed by a treatment of the most important sufi concepts and practices. An examination of sufi institutions, namely the *tekke* and the *tariqat*, concludes this general treatment of sufism.

The second part of the book is a survey of the origins, development, beliefs, and practices of those *tariqats* which had the greatest number of adherents among the Turks of the Ottoman Empire.

Yaşar Nuri Öztürk
Erenköy, Istanbul
May 1988

Contents

Part I

Sufism

Chapter One

The Koran and Sufism

For sufis, as for all Muslims, the Koran is the fundamental guide in matters relating to their religious faith. What distinguishes sufis from other Muslims lies largely in the way they interpret this guide. Sufis advocate an allegorical interpretation of the Koran believing that symbolic or mystical meanings lie concealed beneath its literal sense.

Sufis believe that in order to discover these symbolic meanings one must be able to read the Koran with the "eye of the heart", not with the eyes of one's head. This belief is grounded in the sixth *surah* of the Koran which reads:

> *There is no God save Him, the Creator of all things, so worship Him. He taketh care of all things. The eyes of the head comprehendeth Him not. He comprehendeth all that the eye comprehends. He is subtle. He is aware of all things. In the matter of comprehending God, the eye of the heart has been bestowed by God. And whoever seeth it is for his own good, and whoever is blind is blind to his own hurt.(1)*

The term "eye of the heart" is a metaphor for insight, the ability to see and understand clearly the inner nature and meaning of things. It is, however, a particular kind of insight, one wholly dependent on divine inspiration. Sufis commonly define it as "a power of sight illuminated by a divine light." Among the verses of the Koran which they cite in support of this idea is the following:

> *Light upon light, Allah guideth unto His light whom He will. And Allah speaketh to man in allegories, for Allah is the Knower of all things.(2)*

Nothing is more central to sufism than this "eye of the heart." The practices which comprise the basis of the sufi way of life are all geared toward making this "eye" more receptive to divine illumination.

Sufis have long regarded pride as the greatest obstacle which lies between man and God. They recognize that pride stems from the great pleasure man takes in his own accomplishments. They also recognize that this pleasure is never more intense than when these accomplishments earn him the praise of others. As sufis are called to live their lives not according to their own wills, but in response to divine revelation and inspiration, they regard any sense of personal accomplishment as inimical to their vocation. As divine inspiration often requires sufis to adopt beliefs and practices which conflict with what custom considers fitting and proper, they also look upon the desire for praise as an obstacle to be overcome. In short, sufis regard as most virtuous those who have learned to live without pride.

1

Sufism

In an effort to conquer pride sufis developed a practice called *malamat* (reproach, censure, blame). The sufi practitioner of *malamat* cultivates the habit of self-reproach, as well as the habit of actively avoiding the praise of others. As he does so he takes courage from the following Koranic verse:

> *O ye who believe. Whoever of you becometh a renegade from his religion, (know that in his stead) Allah will bring a people whom he loveth and who love Him, humble toward believers, stern toward disbelievers, striving in the way of Allah, and fearing not the blame of any blamer.(3)*

There are four other practices enjoined by the Koran which, in addition to *malamat,* are regarded as basic to the sufi way of life. The first of these is the practice of *zuhd* (asceticism). The Koran calls upon man to turn away from things passing and provisional that he may be concerned with things eternal and permanent. It issues the following warning:

> *Let not the life of the world beguile you.(4)*

Elsewhere we find these verses:

> *Beautiful for mankind is love of the joys (that come) from women and offspring, and stored-up heaps of gold and silver, and horses branded (with their mark), and cattle and land. That is comfort of the life of the world. Allah! With Him is a more excellent abode.(5)*

> *The life of the world is but a pastime and a game. Lo! The home of the Hereafter, that is life, if they but knew.(6)*

> *Know that the life of this world is only play, and idle talk, and pageantry and boasting among you, and rivalry in respect of wealth and children; as the likeness of vegetation after rain, whereof the growth is pleasing to the husbandman, but afterwards it drieth up and thou seest it turning yellow, then it becometh straw.(7)*

Sufis try to act upon the message of these verses by seeking to live ascetic lives; they endeavor to turn away from the world in order to turn more fully toward God.

Dhikr (remembrance), the second of these four practices, is based in part on the recurrent Koranic injunction, "Remember God often," and on such verses as the following:

> *Verily in the remembrance of Allah do hearts find rest.(8)*

Dhikr usually consists of the mental or verbal repetition of one of the Divine Names or of a verse of the Koran. These prayerful repetitions are often accompanied by physical movements which help the worshipping sufi achieve an ecstatic state. In some instances the movements themselves are regarded as a form of mute *dhikr*. Such is the dance of the Mawlawis, the Whirling Dervishes. *Dhikr* is basically a form of prayer. Sufis believe that by praying in this way they may draw near to God.

The third of these practices is *tahajjud* (praying late at night, especially after midnight). The Prophet Muhammad practiced *tahajjud*. It is a practice based, in part, on the following Koranic verse:

> *Establish worship at the going down of the sun until the dark of night, and (the recital of) the Koran at dawn. Lo! (The recital of) the Koran at dawn is ever witnessed. And some part of the night awake for it, a largesse for thee. It may be that thy Lord will raise thee to a praised estate.(9)*

The fourth of these practices is that of seeking to suffer. Suffering is treated at great length in the Koran. In its pages we frequently encounter the idea that man must suffer in order to find God. The twenty-ninth *surah*, for example, speaks of suffering as follows:

> *Do men imagine that they will be left (at ease) because they say, 'We believe', and will not be tested with affliction? Lo! We tested those who were before you. Thus Allah knoweth those who are sincere, and knoweth those who feign.(10)*

Why is this suffering deemed necessary? Sufis insist that the answer lies in the fact that drawing near to God necessarily entails the painful process of divorcing oneself from all but God. The Koranic story of Abraham and his son Ishmael is often cited by sufis as an example of how difficult this divorce can be. Abu Bakr al-Wasiti (d.322/953) makes the following comments about this story:

> *Allah, in subjecting Abraham to the test of sacrificing his son, intended by this to erase from Abraham's heart the love of all other things. When Abraham looked into his soul, he saw that his son Ishmael was closest to his heart, and he desired his destruction.(11)*

It seems fitting to conclude this brief glance at the relationship between the Koran and sufism with a Koranic passage in which sufis find references and allusions to many of the beliefs and practices which they regard as important, including several of those mentioned above. This famous passage, known as the Light Verse, is as follows:

> *Allah is the Light of the heavens and the earth. The similitude of His light is as a niche wherein is a lamp. The lamp is a glass. The glass*

Sufism

is as it were a shining star. (This lamp is) kindled from a blessed tree, an olive neither of the East or West, whose oil would almost glow forth (of itself) though no fire touched it. Light upon light, Allah guideth unto His light whom He will. And Allah speaketh to mankind in allegories, for Allah is the knower of all things. (This lamp is found) in houses which Allah hath allowed to be exalted and that His name shall be remembered therein. Therein do offer praise to Him at morn and evening men whom neither merchandise nor sale beguileth from remembrance of Allah and constancy in prayer and paying to the poor their due; who fear a day when hearts and eyeballs will be overturned; that Allah may reward them with the best of what they did, and increase reward for them of His bounty. Allah giveth blessings without stint to whom He will. As for those who disbelieve, their deeds are as a mirage in a desert. The thirsty one supposeth it to be water till he cometh unto it and findeth it naught, and findeth, in the place thereof, Allah, Who payeth him his due; and Allah is swift at reckoning. Or as darkness on a vast, abysmal sea. There covereth him in a wave, above which is a wave, above which is a cloud. Layer upon layer of darkness. When he holdeth out his hand he scarce can see it. And he for whom Allah hath not appointed light, for him there is no light. Hast thou not seen that Allah, He it is Whom all who are in the heavens and earth praise, and the birds in their flight? Of each He knoweth verily the worship and the praise; and Allah is aware of what they do. And unto Allah belongeth the sovereignty of the heavens and the earth, and unto Allah is the journeying.(12)

Illustration 1

Illustration 2

Ce huit premières attitudes forment un Rik'ath

MUSULMAN FAISANT LA PRIERE, Namaz.

1 c. p. R.

Illustration 4

8

MUSULMAN FAISANT SON ABLUTION, *Abdellik*

Illustration 5

illustration 7 CALENDÉRY *VOYAGEUR.*

Illustration 8

Chapter Two

The Sunnat and Sufism

The Arabic word *sunnat* means "custom" or "habitual practice". In Islam, it is used to refer to the normative words and deeds of the Prophet Muhammad. The Koran, and the *sunnat* of the Prophet, comprise the foundation of Islamic thought and practice.

There are three different types of *sunnat*: the *sunnat* which is based on the actions of the Prophet; the *sunnat* which is based on the things the Prophet said; and the *sunnat* which sets forth actions of others which, by word or deed, the Prophet either approved or disapproved.

Sufis, like most Muslims, revere the *sunnat* of the Prophet for the light it sheds on the meaning of Koranic revelation. What distinguishes sufis from most other Muslims is the degree of their interest in the *sunnat* for the light it sheds on the life and character of Muhammad, the man whom they take as their model. The Koran says,

> *Verily in the messenger of Allah ye have a good example for him who looketh unto Allah on the Last Day, and remembereth Allah much.(1)*

Sufis believe that Muhammad is the man who most perfectly achieved what they seek: intimacy with God. Thus they believe that by imitating the Prophet's way of life they may be able to attain such intimacy themselves.

Sufis have always been interested in that portion of Muhammad's life which preceded his prophethood, because they believe that his singular greatness of character became apparent early in his life, not just when he became a prophet. In other words, sufis believe that his prophethood instead of radically altering his character, perfected it. They quote the Prophet's biographers who report that the mystical nature of Muhammad's character was apparent well before he became a prophet. These biographers write of his withdrawing to a cave in a hill near Mecca called Hira in order to contemplate. During one of these contemplative sojourns at Hira God began to reveal the Koran to him.

We read that early in his life Muhammad became noted for his righteousness, friendliness, compassion, and pity. People would entrust their most valuable possessions to him, as well as ask him to mediate their disputes. We also read of his behaving in ways which were contrary to those of his fellow Meccans. The rightness of these ways was later confirmed by the Koran. His unique character appears to have impressed all who came in contact with him. His every act reflected the fact that his was a nature that was different. Sufis believe that it was this difference which helped make him a suitable receptacle of divine illumination and the bearer of God's revelation.

After he assumed the mantle of prophecy, Muhammad's actions natural-

Sufism

ly came to be interpreted in the light of his role as the bearer of divine revelation. Of particular interest to sufism in this regard are those of his actions which point beyond the practices prescribed by the Koran for all Muslims; his supererogatory acts of worship. For example, apart from the *salats* (ritual prayer) which all Muslims must perform five times a day, the Prophet would perform additional *salats*, including the *tahajjud* mentioned in the previous chapter. We are told that the Prophet would perform the ritual prayer without interruption for so long that his feet would begin to swell.

Another of the acts of worship prescribed for all Muslims is fasting during the month of Ramadan and on other designated occasions. Here again the Prophet served as a model for sufism in his observance of supererogatory fasts at various times throughout the year. He performed, moreover, some fasts which were prohibited to all but himself, fasts which went on for several consecutive days without the traditional breaking of the fast after sunset.

Sufi piety was thus greatly informed by the supererogation of the Prophet. Sufis also believe that one of the reasons for Muhammad's supererogation was that he wished to show his fellow Muslims ways by which they might sharpen their mystical sensibilities. The most remarkable evidence of the Prophet's concern in this regard is his relationship with the *ahl al-suffah* or the "Companions of the Suffa". Muhammad Hamidullah, one of the outstanding Islamic scholars of our age, describes the significance of the *ahl al-suffah* for sufi history as follows:

> *In the period of the Prophet, in that part of the mosque of Medina where the* salat *was performed, there was an area called the* suffah. *This was a center for education and psychic experimentation which operated under the eye of the Prophet himself. A rather large group of Muslims lived there. These people would pass part of their time in company with others and part in communion with God. To avoid becoming social parasites living freely off the largesse of others, they would also work. They would pass their evenings... performing the late night* salat *(tahajjud), reciting litanies (dhikr), and contemplating.(2)*

As this description of Hamidullah suggests, the Prophet encouraged those of his Companions who wished to engage in supererogatory spiritual exercises. Although sufi scholars have amassed evidence which shows that Muhammad personally advised these Companions as to how they should carry out these exercises, we have no records which indicate precisely what this advice was.

Ascetic practices of an extreme nature are looked on with suspicion by most sufis as being contrary to the Islamic ideal of moderation. Yet Salamah b. Dinar (d.140/757), a man who lived in the time of the Successors to the Prophet, ably replied to those who criticized his extreme ascetic practices by saying:

> *Why should I lighten the burden I have imposed on my flesh. No less than fourteen enemies watch for the chance to assault me. These*

The Sunnat and Sufism

are the devil, jealousy, unbelievers, the two-faced, hunger, thirst, heat, cold, nakedness, old age, sickness, poverty, death, and hell. A power-ful weapon is required by one who would stand against so many enemies. And I have been unable to find a more potent weapon than godliness.(3)

It is clear, however, that the Prophet was opposed to extremism. The following incident might be cited as evidence of this. We read that 'Uthman b. Maz'un asked the Prophet to be allowed to sever relations with his wife. The Prophet replied to his request as follows:

Is my moral example not sufficient for you, 'Uthman? I have rela-tions with women; I eat meat; and, moreover, I keep the fast. You should know that keeping the fast [during which time sexual intercourse is pro-hibited] is the manner of the emasculation of the Muslim community.

Sa'd b. Abu Waqqas on whose authority this *hadith* (narrative relating a deed or utterance of the Prophet) rests, added:

Had not the Prophet prohibited tabattul *[living as a celibate recluse as an act of piety towards God], 'Uthman would have immediately gone and had himself castrated.(4)*

As was made clear in the previous chapter, sufis value highly the ability to discern the profound spiritual meaning which may be contained within an otherwise unremarkable word or action. They claim that from the records of the Prophet's life it is clear that Muhammad believed in such hidden spiritual meanings and that he imparted the secret of discerning them to his Compan-ions. Sufis reckon 'Ali b. Abi Talib, the Prophet's cousin and son-in-law, to have been the greatest of all the Companions. This esteem is partly based on the fact that of all the Companions 'Ali was the one who was best able to discern hidden spiritual meanings. Muhammad spoke of this ability of 'Ali's as follows:

Ey 'Ali! Allah has commanded me to instruct you well in the subtleties of religion so that you will comprehend and so that you will gain a power that will fill your heart. It was for this that the Koranic verse, 'For heeding ears to comprehend', was revealed. And so it is that you have become the power to heed and comprehend fully.(5)

'Ali stands at the head of the spiritual genealogies of almost all sufi schools and is recognized in sufi history as foremost among the *walis* (saints). Abu Bakr, the first caliph, is also among the Companions whom tradition portrays as possessed of a knowledge of the science of mysteries and signs. One day the Prophet reportedly asked him,

Do you remember the day that was no time other than itself?

15

Sufism

To which Abu Bakr responded,

> *Yes, O Emissary of God.*

When his friends later asked him what was meant by the Prophet's cryptic reference, Abu Bakr replied,

> *That day is the day of* mithaq *[the day on which man is with God for all eternity].(6)*

The Prophet often spoke of hidden meanings and of the power to discern them. On one occasion he said:

> *There is a part of knowledge like a pearl set in mother- of-pearl, which only servants with a profound knowledge of God can discern. And when they speak of this knowledge they will not be rejected save by those who overstep themselves in pride and self-centeredness before God.(7)*

On another occasion he said this:

> *Knowledge is twofold: The first part is hidden in the heart and it is this which is useful.(8)*

In order to understand fully the depths of the sufi attachment to Muhammad it is necessary to grasp the sufi concept of *Nur-i Muhammadi* (The Light of Muhammad). One of the most concise statements of this concept is by Jafar al-Sadıq (d.148/765):

> *The very first of God's creations was the light of Muhammad. First among all the handiworks of God were the atoms of Muhammad. And the first thing the divine pen wrote were the words, 'There is no god but Allah and Muhammad is his servant and prophet.'(9)*

Behind this statement lie these words attributed to the Prophet:

> *The first thing that God created was my light.(10)*

The *Nur-i Muhammadi* is thus a divine light, the creation of which preceded the actual coming into the world of Muhammad himself. For this reason sufis believe that Muhammad, in the form of this light, has been a beacon to the world since the beginning of time. This idea is reinforced by the following two *hadith*:

The Sunnat and Sufism

When Adam was between mud and water, I was even then the Prophet.(11)

I came down through the ages sifting and selecting among the various epochs of man and appeared finally in the age in which I now live.(12)

This Light of Muhammad has been the subject of a great many sufi literary works. Perhaps the most famous of these is the *Tawasin* of Hallaj. The following eulogy to this *Nur-i Muhammadi* is an extract from the *Tawasin:*

Muhammad is a lamp lit from the light of eternity, a light which flashed forth and returned to its source. Superior to all lamps, he became the sultan of lamps. He is the moon which shone brightest among the moons and his sign of the zodiac is in the firmament of secrets.... His light sprang up among clouds of doves and his sun shone forth from Mecca.... His lamp took light from the torch of exaltation and nobility.... The light of prophecy radiates from his light alone. Even the radiance of light was from his radiance. There is no light older or clearer than the light of eternity, save only the light of the Prophet, the exalted of the exalted.... His power and exertion are before all exertions. His existence was prior to nothingness and his name before the first stroke of the divine pen. He is prior to all existing things.... He is immortal, he lives always, he remains always as he was.... He was before all events, all matter.... He was the before of all befores and the afterwards of all afters....(13)

The being of Muhammad, as at once the first light and the last prophet, has been expressed by Turkish sufis in this sentence: "He was the first illumination of existence and its last manifestation." The roots of this idea may be traced back to the following *hadith:*

I am the first of men in creation and I am the last to be sent as a prophet.(14)

Sufi thought has concluded from these words that because Muhammad is both the consummate man and the final prophet, all men and all prophets are incipient manifestations of the perfection of his character and wisdom. In the words of one of the "divine *hadith*",

Were it not for you, O Muhammad, I would not have brought creatures into being.(15)

As sufis believe that Muhammad was the perfect man, his life has become for them the standard by which all men must measure themselves. As we have

17

Sufism

already seen, the Koran states this idea in these words:

> *Verily in the messenger of Allah ye have a good example for him who looketh unto Allah and the Last Day, and remembereth Allah much.(16)*

For this reason sufis have tried to attain, within the limits of their capacities, to those qualities evinced by Muhammad. This imitation of the Prophet is carried to great lengths by some sufis. There are, for example, some sufis who refuse to sit with their legs stretched out in front of them, as it is reported that Muhammad never assumed this posture. Other sufis refuse to eat melons. They say that as it is not known how the Prophet ate this fruit, they prefer not to eat it rather than to eat it in a way of which the Prophet might have disapproved.

'Ali b. Abi Talib, the cousin, son-in-law, and Companion of the Prophet, described Muhammad in this way:

> *Muhammad was neither so tall as to offend the eye, nor so short as to attract attention. He was of middle height. His hair was neither tightly curled nor completely straight. It was wavy. His body was not large, neither was it coarse. His face was neither completely round nor unduly small. It was pink approaching white. His eyes were deep black. His lashes long. His joints and shoulder blades were broad. The hair on his chest was sparse, extending down to his navel. The other parts of his body were hairless. His hands and feet were rather large. When he walked, he seemed to step on the tips of his toes; he walked quickly as though running. When he walked it was as though the ground withdrew before him. When he looked in any direction he would turn his whole body. He was never seen to look at something by merely turning his head. Between his shoulders was the seal of prophecy.*
>
> *He was the most generous of men, had the best of hearts, and spoke most truly. No one was seen to display as much loyalty in the things entrusted to him. He was the most mild-tempered of men. He was the easiest of all men to get along with. One who saw him for the first time would tremble before his imposing air, but once with him for a while, would fall in love with him, and would speak of nothing but his allure and charisma. In short, I saw no other man but him who gathered in himself all beauties.(17)*

Muhammad was a man who possessed great spiritual attractiveness. His humility is one of the many virtues which sufis especially esteem.

> *I am not to be compared to a king. I am the son of a woman from the tribe of the Quraish who ate cured meat.(18)*

The Sunnat and Sufism

From this we see that despite the gloriousness of his mission, his exemplary character, and his outstanding mystical sensibilities, Muhammad was yet acutely conscious that, in the final analysis, he was but a mortal man. His superior status as a man derived simply from his having been elevated to be a bearer of God's revelation, and from the manner in which his human qualities accorded with those ideal qualities set forth in this revelation. The Koran recognized and is harshly condemnatory of the human temptation to divinize such personalities. It is clear that Muhammad himself opposed such tendencies among his Companions. He is reported to have given this warning:

Do not praise me as Christians excessively praise Jesus the son of Mary. Know ye that I am the servant and apostle of God. (19)

Sufis are admiring of Muhammad in his role as the servant of God, since the Koran states that serving God is the greatest activity in which a man can be engaged. They see him as someone who served God by acting as a teacher to all mankind. Muhammad himself once described his role as teacher in this way:

I am for you as a father with his children, I will teach and instruct you. (20)

Sufis also believe that he serves Muslims by interceding for them after they have died. They cite the following *hadith* as proof of this:

My life is mercy and a blessing unto you. You will speak in my presence and an answer will be given to you. My passing in death will be mercy and a blessing for you. After I die your actions will be presented to me and I will consider them. If you have performed good deeds, I will praise God. If you have done evil, I will ask God's forgiveness of you. (21)

Sufis believe that such intercession can be performed not only by Muhammad but by the other prophets and saints of Islam as well.

Another basic tenet of sufi thought is that Muhammad's love for a person is greater than that person's love of himself. The following *hadith* has been quoted by sufis in support of this idea:

I am closer to all believers without exception, in their works in this world and the next, than are they themselves, more compassionate. Recite, if it is evidence you seek, this verse of the Koran: "The Prophet is closer to believers than their selves and more compassionate" (...III, 6). Therefore if any believer should die leaving his family in debt or poor, let that family come to me, I am its guardian. (22)

19

Sufism

Sufis regard Muhammad as the foremost of men, the first of the servants of God, and the last and greatest of the Prophets. Although sufis believe that he was the man through whom the light of God has shone most intensely, they do not regard him as the only conveyor of God's light. They express the conviction that he was proceeded as well as followed by a number of lesser servants of God, each of whom has also functioned as a conveyor of this light. These include all those whom sufis regard as having achieved an especial closeness to God, people whom sufis term *walis* (saints).

Finally, it should be noted that, according to a sufi reading of the Koran, the divine light of God can shine in the hearts of those who do not call themselves Muslim. The following Koranic passage has been cited as an illustration of this:

Thou wilt find the nearest of them in affection to those who believe (to be) those who say: Lo! We are Christians. That is because there are among them priests and monks, and because they are not proud. When they listen to what hath been revealed unto the messenger, thou seest their eyes overflow with tears because of their recognition of the Truth. They say: Our Lord, we believe. Inscribe us among thy witnesses. How shall we not believe in Allah and that which hath come unto us as Truth. And (how should we not) hope that our Lord will bring us in along with righteous folk? Allah hath rewarded them for that their saying—Gardens underneath which rivers flow, wherein they will abide forever. This is the reward of the good.(23)

Chapter Three

The Murshid and Zuhd

As we saw in the previous chapter, the sufi is distinguished from other Muslims by the intensity with which he seeks to know God. Those among the earliest Muslims who were exceedingly devoted to the new faith were thus, as it were, the first sufis. The outstanding characteristic of these early devotees was their desire to follow the example of the Prophet as closely as possible. It was this desire which motivated the development of two concepts which are cornerstones of sufi thought; these are the concepts of *murshid* (leader) and *zuhd* (asceticism).

Early sufis believed that Muhammad exemplified life as God wished man to live it. They also believed that by modeling their lives on his they could draw near to God. These beliefs led them to become assiduous students of the *sunnat*. Despite the fact that they helped to produce rich collections of *hadith*, however, they were not satisfied with the model of life which these *hadith* provided.

Sufis overcame this problem by coming to the conviction that Muhammad's spirit actually lived on in others. If, therefore, one knew who these others were, one could look to them as sure guides in matters of religious belief and conduct. These bearers of the spirit of Muhammad were viewed as the supreme living interpreters of the *sunnat*. They were given the title of *murshid* by those who recognized the *Nur-i Muhammadi* which shone from within them.

Once the *murshid* had come to be regarded as the earthly representative of the Prophet, it followed that the sufi who was intent on drawing near to God could do so by following the example of his *murshid*. Sufis cite the following Koranic verses in support of this idea:

Say (O Muhammad, to mankind): If you love Allah, follow me; Allah will love you and forgive your sins.(1)

Lo! those who swear allegiance unto thee (Muhammad) swear allegiance only unto Allah. The hand of Allah is above their hands....(2)

Swearing allegiance to a *murshid* thus became equivalent to swearing allegiance to the Prophet, and consequently to God. Sufis came to regard a true *murshid* as one who could be said to have been annihilated in the Prophet and thus in God. By this they meant that just as God has been the motivator of all the Prophet's words and deeds so also was He the motivator of all the true *murshid* said and did.

When a *murid* (disciple, novice) put himself under the direction of a *murshid*, he was embarking on a process which sufis began to describe as a "se-

Sufism

cond birth''. This term may well have originated with the following words of Jesus:

> *Truly, truly, I say unto you, unless one is born anew, he cannot see the Kingdom of God.(3)*

Sufis found the idea of a second birth to be implicit in this Koranic verse:

> *Journey in the land, then behold how He originated creation, then God caused a second growth to grow.(4)*

They also found this idea in the following *hadith*:

> *Die before you die.(5)*

As time passed sufi writers tried to analyze this idea of a second birth in various ways. They were united, for the most part, in regarding the natural world as a metaphorical womb in which human beings receive their earliest nurture. The *murshid* was then viewed as a metaphorical father (sometimes mother), a person through whom God works to bring humanity to true maturity. The idea of rebirth was reflected in the terms "child of the heart" and "child of the Way" (i.e. the Sufi Way), both of which were used as synonymous for *murid*.

As a child inherits through its parents those traits peculiar to its ancestors, so a *murid* through his *murshid* was thought to inherit the traits of his spiritual ancestors. These ancestors extended back along a line of *murshids* which culminated in the Prophet himself. From the Prophet the ancestral line extended directly to God. The unbroken chain of these spiritual ancestors was termed a *silsilah*. The sufi Imam Rabbani (d.1031/1621) expressed this idea as follows:

> *The child of the heart is the spiritual heir. As spiritual heir he inherits faith and knowledge of God in the spiritual realm as opposed to material goods. He is thus the heir of the prophets and saints in this second sense.(6)*

Rabbani was echoing these two sayings of the Prophet:

> *Scholars are heirs of the prophets.*

> *We the prophets have no heirs. All the goods we leave are alms.(7)*

In other words, the heir of the prophets was thought to inherit spiritual knowledge and values, not material goods.
'Abd al-Wahid b. Zayd (d.177/793) said,

The Murshid and Zuhd

A believer in this world may be likened to a fetus in the womb.
Such is the believer. At first he dreads leaving the world; but once he
has left it, he never wishes to return to it.(8)

Sufis came to believe that once the *murid* had experienced spiritual rebirth he would no longer regard this world's values as ultimate. He would continue to live in this world, but not as he had previously lived; because his spirit, having experienced something infinitely better, would no longer be able to take sustenance from the material values this world exalts. The Turkish poet Fuzuli (d.964/1556) wrote:

Fallen now into a sea of love, forget ye now
thy life of precious stones,

Your spirit has returned home, forget ye now the taste of
blood in the womb consumed.

For sufis the sea has long been a symbol of God. They have believed that the human soul, consciously or unconsciously, seeks to be reunited with God its maker, just as a river seeks the sea. God, like the sea, can receive and cleanse the polluted waters of many rivers without Himself becoming polluted. The *murshid* is the mouth of many rivers connecting human souls to the Divine sea. Abu Sa'id Ibn Abi'l-Khayr (d.1132), described the ideal *murshid* as follows:

1) He should be an example such that his disciples may
be guided through observation of him.
2) He should have received the training of the tariqat
that he be enabled to thus train others.
3) He should be adorned with manners and moral beauty so that
he may impart them to others.
4) He should be possessed of generosity so that he may use his
belongings for the benefit of his disciples.
5) He should not covet the possessions of his disciples and thus
create obstacles between himself and them.
6) He should not impart verbally advice which he can impart by
means of signs.
7) He should not undertake to train people by means of violence or
wrath when gentleness will suffice.
8) He should have done himself whatever he advises others to do.
9) He should himself avoid all things that he has forbidden to
others.
10) He should not abandon for the sake of man that disciple whom
he has accepted for the sake of God.(9)

Sufism

Ahmad Rif'at (d.1876), writing about the ideal *murshid*, had this to say:

1) *Under all circumstances he should be orthodox in his ways.*
2) *He should understand the esoteric sciences so as to avoid inappropriate interpretations of events submitted to him.*
3) *He should engage in sweet and friendly conversation with dervishes and possess perfection and intelligence.*
4) *He should be generous.*
5) *He should be courageous and submit to none but God.*
6) *He should eschew lust and avoid women.*
7) *He should not harbor love for this world nor covet the goods of his dervishes, nor, except under conditions of necessity, engage in farming, etc..*
8) *He should behave with compassion toward his disciples.*
9) *He should have a mild disposition.*
10) *He should be forgiving.*
11) *His morals should be outstanding.*
12) *He should not employ his disciples in private matters when they occupied with their own.*
13) *He should be noble, spiritually distinguished, manly, and reliable.*
14) *He should have placed himself fully in the hands of God.*
15) *He should have achieved a state of surrender and obedience to the will of God.*
16) *He should evince submission in the face of accidents and fate.*
17) *He should possess gravity and be a man of his word.*
18) *He should be calm and unhurried.*
19) *Having once decided on a course of action, he should not turn back from what he has resolved to do.(10)*

'Ali b. Abi Talib, the cousin and son-in-law of the Prophet, is included in the *silsilahs* of all Turkish sufis. He is, after Muhammad, the prototypical *murshid* and therefore some special note of 'Ali and his place in sufi tradition is in order. We may begin by noting that 'Ali is remembered in Islamic sources as the first male to have believed in Muhammad's prophetic mission. While still a boy 'Ali went to live with Muhammad. He married Muhammad's daughter Fatima, a union which added two grandsons to the household of the Prophet. From the sufi standpoint, the importance of these facts derives mainly from their pointing to the intimacy of 'Ali's association with Muhammad. Sufis came to believe that no other person was better positioned than 'Ali to receive the stamp of Muhammad's personality and to pass it on to select members of the next generation of Muslims.

The Murshid and Zuhd

Sufis regard 'Ali as a man of outstanding spiritual qualities. It was no doubt because of these qualities that 'Ali became drawn to the Prophet, and there is no doubt that these qualities helped 'Ali to gain favor in the Prophet's eyes. The extent of the Prophet's esteem for 'Ali can be measured by two *hadith*: According to the first of these, the Prophet said,

> *I am the city of knowledge and 'Ali is the gate to the city. Therefore let him who desires knowledge approach that gate.(11)*

According to the second, he said,

> *I am the house of wisdom, 'Ali is the door.(12)*

Zuhd—Toward the close of the era known in Muslim history as the Age of the Companions of the Prophet,(13) sufis began to place more emphasis on *zuhd* (asceticism). This was largely motivated by the fact that the Muslim political world of the Umayyads (661/750) and 'Abbasids (750/1258) was, by comparison with that of the Prophet, worldly and corrupt. The splendor of the caliphal courts at Damascus and Baghdad was certainly a far cry from the Spartan simplicity in which Muhammad and 'Ali had lived. The intrigue which characterized these courts stood in marked contrast to the openness of Muhammad and his Companions. Sufis began feeling that they were living in a world which was abandoning true Islam. In protest against this they turned to pious asceticism.

For these sufis *zuhd* basically meant turning one's back on all but God. They came to feel that such complete devotion to God could be accomplished in two stages. In the first stage the sufi was to abstain from all worldly things in excess of those which are vital. In the second stage he was to purge himself of all desires apart from those which lead him to God. It goes without saying that the second stage was the more difficult, the heart being more difficult to tame than the body.

Once the taming of the heart had been achieved, the sufi was ready to begin life anew. In this new life the sufi actually returned to the world he had abandoned in order to turn his fellow men, who live in the world according to worldly desires, toward God. This end sometimes required the sufi to become, once again, the possessor of goods and power. If so, the sufi could accept this requirement with confidence, as he knew that he would be able to use these things selflessly to serve God. As these worldly things no longer had the power to command his heart, he could use them as instruments of creation rather than destruction.

At this point mention should be made of two important sufi concepts: *fana* and *baqa*.(14) *Fana* can mean "annihilation", "obliteration" or "extinction". Sufis came to use the word to refer to a human soul's becoming annihilated in that instant when it encounters God directly. A favorite sufi

Sufism

metaphor for this experience depicts a moth, which represents the human soul, circling a candle flame, which represents God. The moth circles irresistibly closer and closer to the flame until it is suddenly immolated in the all-consuming glory of its light. Sufis know that in that instant when the soul encounters God it is so overcome by His all-consuming Presence that all consciousness of things apart from God melts into an ecstatic feeling of oneness with Him; the soul enters a state known as *fana*.

Sufis began using the term *baqa* (abiding, remaining) to refer to a man's abiding in God after he has emerged from the state of *fana*. God first annihilates the believer and then, if his spiritual state is sufficiently advanced, returns him to consciousness, but to a consciousness which has been radically transformed. A man in a state of *baqa*, though once again separated from God, and active in the world, is still so closely in touch with Him that all his acts are informed, not by his own ego, but by God's will. Sufis discovered that by taming their hearts through the practice of *zuhd* they could attain these states.

Written works treating *zuhd* began to appear from the first century onward. Among the earliest of these are the letters of Hasan al- Basri (d.110/728), the poems of Sabiq b. 'Abdillah al-Barbari (d.c. 100/718), and *al-Sahifah fi al-Zuhd* (The Sheet Concerning Asceticism) by Sabiq b. 'Abdillah al-Husayn (d. 92/710). Other comparatively early works were written by the great ascetic and traditionist 'Abd Allah b. al-Mubarak (d. 181/797), the traditionist and historian, Asad b. Musa al-Umawi (d.212/827), and the great legal scholar, Ahmad b. Hanbal (d.241/855).

Chapter Four

The Rise of the Tekke

Muslims have always viewed the period which encompassed the lifetime of the Prophet as the golden age of Islam, the time when those who called themselves Muslim actually lived their lives in close accordance with the laws which God had ordained for them. This situation soon changed, however, owing to the military conquests which made the Muslims rulers of a great empire. The result of this, as has been mentioned earlier, was a gradual abandonment of the standards ordained by God. Although most people still paid lip service to these standards they had ceased to live their lives in accordance with them. As a protest against this situation sufis began to emphasize the practice of asceticism. It was in this setting that the institution known as the *tekke* (place of repose, refuge, asylum) was to develop.

The great nineteenth-century Turkish sufi, Kuşadalı İbrahim Khalwati, offered the following explanation for the origin of the *tekke*:

> *In early times, progress along the path to God was made by means of ghaza....(1) Later, (ghaza was eclipsed by) greed for territory and became impractical. At this point, in order to sustain a movement along the path to God, kindred spirits began to meet in large houses and in rural areas. Gradually, because these places, too, were effected by disturbances, tekkes were formed....(2)*

This explanation merits some consideration. In it Kuşadalı is saying that in the time of the Prophet, Muslims strove to draw nearer to God by living as he commanded. Later, especially in Ummayad and 'Abbasid times, the desire for conquests and material gain began to displace the desire to draw near to God. As greed distorted the hearts of Muslims, so it distorted the institutions which gave order to their lives. If once participation in the institutions of the Muslim community led toward God, now such participation led toward the world and away from God. The *tekke* thus came into being as a place of refuge from the corruption and hypocrisy of this world.

It is widely accepted that the first *tekke* was founded in Damascus in the year 150/767.(3) *Tekkes* were next seen in Irak and Khorasan. Before long they had spread throughout the Islamic world and had paved the way for the great sufi brotherhoods or *tariqats* of a later age for which they were to constitute the nuclei.

Tekkes were places of prayer and worship. Yet they often functioned secondarily as academies of the Islamic sciences, missionary organizations, institutions exercising influence over local economic decisions, fine arts academies, sources of military support,(4) and, of far-reaching significance, as an important stimulus for the development of *waqifs*.

Sufism

Waqifs were endowments of property, in the main, real estate, the yield of which was to be used for specified pious purposes. As institutions designed to reconstitute the golden age of Islam in which all life was lived in pilgrimage along the path to God, the *tekkes* became the objects of many such endowments. Throughout the Islamic world the spread of *tekkes* went hand in hand with an increase in the number of *waqifs*. The *tekke-waqif* duality became the wellspring of a new spiritual wealth and of public services throughout the Islamic world.(5)

The *zawiyah* and the *ribat* were each a special kind of *tekke*. The *zawiyah* was a small *tekke* often established on a crossroads and served as a place where dervishes could break their journeys. *Zawiyahs* became important elements in the communication networks of the Seljuk and Ottoman Empires. The *ribats* were originally established as frontier outposts. The word *ribat* means a place where *murabatah* (keeping watch for enemies along the borders)(6) was carried out.(7) At some point they became *tekkes* as well. They were inhabited by both soldiers and sufis, the latter's duty being to look after the spiritual welfare of the former. In later times these two charges were combined into one and there emerged a group of dervishes called the *alp-erenler* (lit. enlightened heroes) who did battle with both sword and soul. The *ribats* were considered of great importance by both Seljuk and Ottoman rulers. The Seljuk vizir Nizam al- Mulk made "the establishment of *ribats* along important roads" one of the central tasks of his administrators.(8)

Tekkes were usually built in a simple, unostentatious style. All *tekkes*, however small, contained one large room used for gatherings of various sorts. This room was called the *sama'hana* and was used for the performance of the *dhikr*. The *sama'hana* was also used for the performance of the *salat*, the ritual prayer which Muslims are required to perform five times a day. The larger *tekkes* usually contained additional rooms. Some *sama'hanas*, for example, might have contained a section where musicians could sit while they played a musical accompaniment for the *dhikr*. In some *tekkes* one might also have found separate living quarters reserved for the sheikh (head) of the *tekke*, as well as a separate living area reserved for the sheikh's wife, daughters, and small sons. Some *tekkes* also contained *hujras* (cells), single rooms made to accommodate those sufis who lived at the *tekke*. Some *tekkes* which engaged in benevolent activities contained either rooms or separate buildings where activities could be carried out. The Miskinler Tekkesi in Istanbul, for example, was known for its large hospital for lepers.

The *chilakhana* was a place within the *tekke* complex where *chila* (a forty-day period of solitary contemplation) was carried out. The successful completion of this forty day period of contemplation came to be required by almost all *tekkes* as a prerequisite for membership. This period of solitary contemplation involved much suffering. In everyday Turkish the word *çile* (derived from the Persian word *chila*) has come to mean "ordeal", "suffering", "enduring hardship".

Illustration 9

Illustration 10

Illustration

Illustration 12 TSCHILLE 33

OU PÉNITENCE PARTICULIERE DES DERWISCHS.

Lithog.ᵉ en Couleurs par A.Bayot.

DERWI

Illustration 13

Imp de Prick et 20 r et pas 8 Sorbonne Paris

TOURNEURS

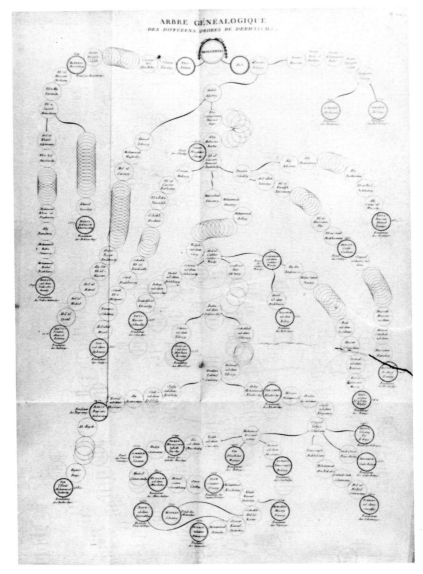

Illustration 14

The Rise of the Tekke

The *murid* who entered upon this process was called in Turkish *ıkrar vermiş kişi* (one who has committed himself to God and his *murshid*). If he was young, the *tekke* had to get the permission of the *murid's* family before allowing him to undertake his *chila*. The nature of the ordeal was explained to both the *murid* and his guardians and then a three-day trial was often conducted. The trial period was spent with the novice kneeling on an animal hide in a place just outside the *chilakhana*. He had to remain on this skin with his head bowed throughout this entire three-day period. He was permitted to break this posture only if his *murshid* or his bodily functions required that he do so.

If his *murshid* asked him to break this posture, it would be to make him undergo tests of another kind. These tests were designed to gauge his patience and his trustworthiness. One of these tests might well be to send the *murid* to a distant part of the town to buy, let us say, some fruit. He would be given very detailed instructions as to how to carry this errand out. He might then be followed to make sure he carried out the task as instructed. Even if he carried out the errand as instructed and returned with the fruit, the *murshid* might pretend that the fruit was imperfect and thus require that he go back and exchange it. These trials had very old precedents. We know, for example, that Dhunnun al-Misri (d. 245/859) gave one of his *murids* a box in which he had placed a mouse. He instructed the *murid*, who had no knowledge of the box's contents, to take the box to a distant village without, under any circumstances, opening it. In the course of the long journey, however, the *murid* was overcome by curiosity and opened the box, whereupon the mouse escaped. When the young man returned, Dhunnun said to him,

We entrusted you with a mouse and you betrayed even him. This being so, how can we entrust you with divine secrets. Be gone with you.(9)

If by his own request the *murid* opted to withdraw from the ordeal, or if he failed a test, he was dubbed in Turkish *çilesini kırdı* (one who has broken his ordeal). Having raised questions about his character by breaking his ordeal, the *murid* would find difficulty persuading the *murshid* to allow him another trial.

Chapter Five

Three Great Sufi Thinkers

The conclusion of the creative period in other branches of Islamic thought may be roughly dated toward the end of the second Islamic century. This was not, however, the end of sufism's inventive age. Sufi thinkers were able to sustain their creativity for at least another three centuries. Surveying sufism's creative period as a whole, three names stand out. They are Junayd al-Baghdadi (d.297/909), who raised the great issues of sufism, Abu Hamid al-Ghazzali (d.585/1111), who effected a synthesis of sufism with Sunni theology and law, and Ibn al-'Arabi (d.639/1240), who may be credited with an analogous synthesis of sufism and philosophy.

Annemarie Schimmel called Junayd the undisputed master of the Sufis of Baghdad and the pivotal personality of sufism's classic age.(1) This man, whose full name was Junayd b. Muhammad Abu'l-Qasım al-Khazzaz al-Qawariri, was the scion of a Persian family which had settled in Baghdad. He studied sufism under his uncle, Sari al-Saqati, one of the most revered sufis of the period.

Junayd was instructed by many of the greatest scholars of his age. He had a great respect for the *shari'at*, (the body of Islamic law based on the Koran and the *sunnat* of the Prophet). His efforts to ground sufi principles in the Koran and the *hadith* won for sufism a hearing even among those who were most hostile to it. Ibn Taymiyah, at once one of history's staunchest defenders of Sunni thought and one of sufism's most redoubtable foes, pronounced Junayd the supreme exemplar of the "true *wali* (saint) and friend of God". Abu Hamid al-Ghazzali and Ibn al-Arabi were both greatly influenced by his writings.

In Junayd's thought *tawhid* (the oneness of God) is concretely apprehended through entering a state of *fana*. According to him, the experience of *fana* is the pinnacle of man's spiritual ascent. It is, however, a pinnacle which has its foundation in the *shari'at*. Junayd said this about sufism:

> Our science is built on the solid foundation of the Book (Koran) and the sunnat. He who has not memorized the Koran, does not live the hadith, and does not concern himself with the law; he cannot be considered a practitioner of our science.(2)

He believed that it was essential to be able to demonstrate a correspondence between mystical insight and the *shari'at*. When mystical insight conflicts with the *shari'at* it must be considered erroneous. Junayd expressed his position in these words:

> The disappearance of ecstasy in the authoritative dicta of the shari'at is to be preferred over the disappearance of the shari'at in ecstasy.(3)

Three Great Sufi Thinkers

One of Junayd's most outstanding contributions to sufi thought was his theory of the *mithaq* (Primeval Covenant). According to this theory the souls of men, prior to their endowment with finite existence, swore an oath of fealty to God on behalf of all the generations of men to follow. In return for this God endowed human souls with separate and individual existences. Owing to this primeval oath of fealty, there exists a subliminal urge in the hearts of all men to return to their original home in God. Junayd thought the purpose of sufi education was to bring man to an awareness of this urge. This awareness would then facilitate man's return to God; it would, as Junayd put it, "cause man to attain to his original and pure state."

Ghazzali was one of the greatest systematic thinkers the Islamic world ever produced. His stature among sufis may be judged by his title "The Proof of Islam". Ghazzali was born into an age of military turmoil and intellectual ferment. The Sunni 'Abbasid caliph, who had his court in Baghdad, was engaged in a bitter struggle with the Shi'ite Fatimids, who had set up a caliphate of their own in Cairo. Had it not been for the Seljuk Turks, it is quite likely that the Fatimids would have conquered Baghdad and abolished the 'Abbasid caliphate completely. In the intellectual realm Sunni thinkers found themselves under attack by the Shi'ite Ismailis, whose base was the famous school of al-Azhar in Cairo.

After Ghazzali appeared upon the scene, however, the Sunnis emerged as the victors in this intellectual war. Ghazzali was a sufi who was intimately acquainted with the theology and the juridical sciences of Islam. His great accomplishment was to effect a synthesis of these sciences and sufism. To this day sufis regard this synthesis as the classic outline of their position within the framework of Sunni Islam. While making this synthesis Ghazzali criticized the Sunni jurists for neglecting to take into account the mystical side of man, and brilliantly exposed the errors of the Ismailis. Ghazzali's most famous work is the *Ihya' ulum al-din* (The Revival of the Religious Sciences).

In 488/1095, Ghazzali had a conversion experience which led him to give up academic life and live the life of a sufi for ten years. In the following passage from his autobiographical work, *al-Munqidh min al- dalal* (Deliverer from Error), he gives voice to some of the thoughts which led him to live as a sufi and motivated him to undertake a synthesis of sufi and juridical-theological thought in his *Ihya'ulum al- din*.

> Then I turned my attention to the Way of the Sufis. I knew that it could not be traversed to the end without both doctrine and practice, and that the gist of the doctrine lies in overcoming the appetites of the flesh and getting rid of its evil dispositions and vile qualities, so that the heart may be cleared of all but God; and the means of clearing it is dhikr Allah, i.e. commemoration of God and concentration of every thought upon Him. Now, the doctrine was easier to me than the practice, so I began by learning their doctrine from the books and sayings

Sufism

of their Shaykhs, until I acquired as much of their Way as it is possible to acquire by learning and hearing, and saw plainly that what is most peculiar to them cannot be learned, but can only be reached by immediate experience and ecstasy and inward transformation. I became convinced that I had now acquired all the knowledge of Sufism that could possibly be obtained by means of study; as for the rest, there was no way of coming to it except by leading the mystical life. I looked on myself as I then was. Worldly interests encompassed me on every side. Even my work as a teacher—the best thing I was engaged in—seemed unimportant and useless in view of the life hereafter. When I considered the intention of my teaching, I perceived that instead of doing it for God's sake alone I had no motive but the desire for glory and reputation. I realized that I stood on the edge of a precipice and would fall into Hell-fire unless I set about to mend my ways.... Conscious of my helplessness and having surrendered my will entirely, I took refuge with God as a man in sore trouble who has no resources left. God answered my prayer and made it easy for me to turn my back on reputation and wealth and wife and children and friends.(3)

Ibn al-'Arabi, known to sufis as *al-Shaykh al- akbar* (The Greatest Master), was similar to Ghazzali in that his genius lay partly in his ability to systematize and synthesize the insights of earlier thinkers. He was raised in Spain where his father was a civil servant of high rank in the city of Seville. He was thoroughly familiar with the works of the great Islamic thinkers, including those who propounded heretical views. Ibn al-'Arabi became a sufi when he was about twenty years old. He spent much of the rest of his life traveling throughout the Islamic world. These travels took him to Anatolia where he was received by the Seljuk sultan as an honored guest. It is said that while he was in Malatya he gave lessons to Sadruddin Qonawi, the man who was to become the foremost interpreter of his thought.

Referring to a divine *hadith*, Ibn al-'Arabi said that God created the world because He was a hidden treasure who wished to be known. The universe came into existence to manifest God and is sustained from moment to moment by God's desire to become more fully manifest. All things are created in accordance with forms or archetypes which have existed in God's knowledge from all eternity. Existing things, including human souls, can achieve fulfillment only by turning in worship toward those forms which they were created to represent on earth, forms which are intermediary between God and creation.

As it was God's desire to be known which gave birth to the universe, the universe serves as a mirror which reflects the divine attributes. This desire to be known is also reflected in the desire of human souls to know God. Ibn al-'Arabi believed that it is this desire which draws man to God and illuminates the path which man must travel in order to reach God.

An outstanding feature of Ibn al-'Arabi was his readiness to derive insights from even the most heretical of Islamic thinkers, from the different schools of Islamic thought, and also from the other religions of man. According to him all men have been assigned different paths along which they must travel to reach God. For example, Christians have the path of Christianity, and Jews the path of Judaism. The following poem attributed to Ibn al-'Arabi has often been cited as an example of his open tolerance:

There was a time when I took it amiss in my companion if
his religion was not near mine;

But now my heart takes on every form; it is a pasture for
gazelles, a monastery for monks,

A temple of idols and a ka'ba for pilgrims, the tables of the
Torah and the holy book of the Koran.

Whichever way its riding beasts turn, that way lies my religion
and belief.(4)

Chapter Six

The Tariqats

Tariq is an Arabic word meaning "way". The word *tariqat* is derived from *tariq* and may mean variously "moral quality", "sect", "state", "attitude" or "the mark on something". (1) In the Koran, the word *tariqat* can mean "manner", "way", "method", "sect", "religion" or "moral character".(2) In time the word *tariqat* came to mean the "manner", "way" and "moral character" of an exemplary person. Among sufis the word came to denote "the manner and attitude proper to those who enter upon the path to God."(3) Finally, the word *tariqat* came to signify a group of people traveling together on the same path to God, in other words, a sufi brotherhood or dervish order.

In sufi literature the term *tariqat* has always been used in conjunction with *shari'at*, a word which technically means "the road to the watering place". According to sufis the *shari'at* symbolizes the broad way along which mankind must travel in order to find God. Within the confines of this broad way, however, there are many narrower paths, each of which is a *tariqat*. Ideally, each sufi is called upon to travel that path which best suits his temperament. As there are various kinds of human temperaments, so there are various kinds of *tariqats*. This diversity was one reason for the success of the *tariqats*.(4)

As the *tariqats* began to attract great numbers of new adherents to sufism, both within the borders of the Islamic rule and beyond,(5) sufis were confronted with the problem of how to train these new *murids* in the ways of sufism. In former times *murshids* had been able to closely and personally supervise the training of each *murid*. The training of these *murids* could be tailored to suit their individual needs. This had been possible because, with only a small number of *murids*, a *murshid* had the time to become intimately acquainted with each of his *murids*. This, however, was not possible in a situation in which a vast number of *murids* confronted a small number of *murshids*. The sufis in the *tariqats* chose to solve this problem first by making the successful performance of a series of actions the criteria for initiation, and second by abandoning the effort to adapt their methods of training to the unique needs of each initiate; initiates were now expected to adapt themselves to a more or less fixed pattern of spiritual exercises laid down by each *tariqat* for all its adherents.

As competition between *tariqats* for adherents increased, the quality of the spiritual guidance offered by *murshids* was further eroded. Practices gradually came into being which were clearly opposed to the principles and practices of earlier sufis. Many *murshids*, spurred on by the enthusiasm of their adherents, encouraged an exaltation of their spiritual gifts. The *baraka* (spiritual gifts) of these *murshids* came to be regarded with such awe that the *murshids* were, in effect, elevated to a status high above that of ordinary mortals. Their actions thus became virtually beyond criticism. At the same time many *murshids* began to delegate their sons as the inheritors of their *baraka*. This practice was at complete variance with the whole idea of *baraka*. Spiritual gifts, by their very nature, are acquired only by the grace of God, not by blood inheritance.

The word "sufi" is derived from the Arabic word *suf* (wool). There are many *hadith* which enjoin the practice of wearing wool as a sign of pious asceticism. One of these reports that "works of pride are absent in one who wears wool, eats barley bread, and travels on a donkey."(6) Anas b. Malik (d.91/709) reported that "the Prophet used to accept even the invitation of a slave, he used to mount a donkey and he wore wool." Woolen garments became with time an early form of sufi uniform. There was, however, a reaction to this development. Early sufis expressed opposition to external displays of piety believing that the value of asceticism lay not in winning the approval of others, but in turning from the world toward God. Sufyan al-Thawri (d.161/777) reported an incident which sums up the classical sufi position on external displays of piety and especially on distinctive clothing. He once asked Ja'far al- Sadiq (d.148/765),

Why do you wear such expensive clothing?

Ja'far al-Sadiq, revealing a woolen garment worn hidden beneath his external clothing, replied,

This you see above is for man, this below is for God. We hide that which is for God and display that which is for man.(7)

Abandoning this classical sufi position the *tariqats* came to place great emphasis on dress. Each *tariqat* came to possess its distinctive form of *taj* (dervish hat, literally "crown"). This *taj*, together with the *khirka* (dervish cloak), *pashtamal* (sash), and *kamar* (belt) came to constitute the distinguishing marks of most sufis in the *tariqat* period.

Finally, the wealth which in time began to be bestowed on the *tekkes* came to be a detriment instead of a blessing. This money enabled adherents of the *tariqats* to build comfortable quarters for themselves. These comfortable buildings, however, did not abet adherents in their search for God. On the contrary, their comfort only made it harder for them to forget the world and its allurements.

Despite these developments, however, the *tariqats* continued to produce sincere *murshids* with outstanding spiritual gifts and many dedicated *murids*. Where the combination of gifted *murshid* and dedicated *murid* existed, so also did the combination of guidance and discipline necessary to make real progress along the paths to God laid down by the founders of the *tariqats*.

Various attempts have been made to classify these paths or *tariqats*. Bursevi (d.1137/1724) suggested that each *tariqat* might be put into one of three general categories. These were the *tariq-i akhyar* (the Path of the Select and Good);

Sufism

tariq-i abrar (the Path of Maturity of Heart and Those Who Strive for Spiritual Perfection); and *tariq-i shuttar* (the Way of Those Possessed of Ecstasy and Love).

1. Tariq-i akhyar —*This was the path trod by the Successors of the Prophet and those who followed them. Those who, after long struggle, perfect their spirits along this path and arrive at God by its methods, are few in number. Those who set out along this path occupy themselves with good and benevolent works.... Another name for this path is the Way of Pious Asceticism. This is not the path of love. This being so, it is time-consuming. Seekers who choose this path and its methods traverse in thirty years the distance covered in three by love. Even this, however, is no mean accomplishment. Many end their lives without having set out along the path [to God].*

2. Tariq-i abrar —*Those who set out along this path are persons who struggle to acquire exemplary characters, to purify their hearts, to polish them and enlighten their inner worlds. They take as their aim the cleansing of their hearts of all but God.... In this way they acquire divine knowledge. We observe that those overly preoccupied with fasting and worship cannot acquire this (divine knowledge). (However), more reach God by this path than by the previous one....*

3. Tariq-i shuttar —*This path is the way of those possessed of love, ecstasy and affection. (Pilgrims along this path) progress toward God.... Those who set out upon this path, set out at a more advanced stage of the journey than the most advanced one achievable by those pursuing the other paths.... This select path (can be taken only by one in whom) the will has been extinguished. They have heeded the Prophet's command, 'Die before you die' (Ajluni, 2/402).... Voluntary death means to sever all one's ties to the world. Those who live in this state are aware of nothing, not even the existence of their own bodies....(8)*

Attempts were also made to distinguish *tariqats* according to methods employed. For example, a distinction was made between *tariq-i ruhani* (the Way of Spiritual Exaltation), and *tariq-i nafsani* (the Way of Purification of the Self).

1. Tariq-i ruhani —*Believers go to God by means of the spirit. This approach requires no fasting or suffering. This is the easiest path. Upon the exaltation of the spirit, the person is dominant over his body and the reign of the self comes to an end. Therefore, for one able to exalt the spirit there is no need to struggle with the self. For the exaltation of the spirit is effected not by means of dieting and suffering, but by the spiritual power of the* murshid ....(9)

2. Tariq-i nafsani—*This path is the way of those who take as their method the subjugation of the carnal self to the authority of the spirit, a method which entails passing through seven stages:*

- *a) The Stage of the* nafs-i ammarah *(self that is a slave to fleshly desires);*
- *b) The Stage of the* nafs-i lawwamah *(self that is inclined to self-reproach);*
- *c) The Stage of the* nafs-i mulhamah *(self that has been inspired by God);*
- *d) The Stage of the* nafs-i mutmainnah *(self marked by assurance);*
- *e) The Stage of the* nafs-i radiyah *(self marked by willingness);*
- *f) The Stage of the* nafs-i mardiyah *(self with which God is content);*
- *g) The Stage of the* nafs-i zakiyah *(self that is sinless).(10)*

It is now generally accepted that the first *tariqat* was probably founded in the twelfth century A.D. by 'Muhyiddin 'Abdulqadir b. 'Abdallah al-Gilani. It became known as the Qadiri *tariqat*. The Yesevi *tariqat* founded by Ahmad Yesevi, was also established in this century, as was the Rifa'i *tariqat*. Our concern in the second part of this book will be with the major *tariqats* of Anatolia and the Balkans, namely the Yesevis, the Bektashis, the Mawlawis, the Khalwatis, the Qadiris, the Nakshbandis, the Rifa'is, and two *tariqats* in the Malami tradition. We shall now consider each of these in turn, though in addition we will consider the *akhi* associations, groups which bore some resemblance to the *tariqats*.

Part II

The Major Tariqats
of
Anatolia and the Balkans

Chapter Seven

The Yesevis

Any history of the Turkish *tariqats* must begin with Ahmad Yesevi, a Turk who lived in the twelfth century in that part of Persia known as Khorasan. Although the date of his birth remains unknown, we do know that his father was one Sheikh Ibrahim and his mother one Aysha Hatun. She was the daughter of one of Sheikh Ibrahim's disciples. Ahmad Yesevi received his earliest education in Yesi where he became a disciple of Arslan Baba, a *murshid* of some renown in that area. After Arslan Baba's death, he went to Bukhara, where he continued his studies. While there he became a *murid* of the famous *murshid*, Yusuf Hamadhani (d.535/1140). After the death of Hamadhani, Ahmad Yesevi remained in Bukhara for some time before he returned to settle in his native Yesi. There he lived out the rest of his days as a *murshid*, gathering about him a large following.

It is said that Ahmad Yesevi was so intent upon imitating the Prophet Muhammad in all things that he wished to die, as the Prophet had, at the age of sixty-three. With this in mind he had a tomblike, underground cell built for himself. On his sixty-third birthday he entered this cell, having vowed that he would not leave it for the rest of his life. As the date of his birth is unknown, we do not know how long he actually lived in this *chilakhana*. Yesevi died in 1165.

Ahmad Yesevi's tomb was built at the behest of Timur (d.808/1405), the well-known fourteenth century conqueror. Yesevi is said to have spoken to Timur in a dream, saying,

> Go immediately to Bukhara. The death of the ruler is by your hand.(1)

Timur, acting on this advice, attacked Bukhara and found that it fell to him with lightning speed. Out of gratitude for this victory he had a magnificent tomb erected over Yesevi's grave in Yesi.

Yesevi wrote a book of poems known as the *Diwan-i hikmat*. Each poem in the book is a piece of *hikmat* (wisdom) . All of them were written in Turkish, using meters suited to the short vowels of Turkish. They are hymns to divine love, that love which caused God to bring man into being and which causes man to long to return to his home in God.

If we look at Yesevi's *Diwan-i hikmat* we find that it disproves the claim of Fuad Köprülü and others that the founders of Turkish sufism were heavily influenced by Shi'ite Persian sufis. Yesevi's poems reveal him to have been a sufi who possessed a great respect for the *shari'at*. They betray no sign that the author had been much influenced by Shi'ite Persian thought.

The following poems have been selected from the *Diwan-i hikmat*:

The Major Tariqats

Wherever thou seest the broken heart, be thou a salve that
mends.
If any oppressed on the road remains, be thou an intimate
friend.
Be thou a salve to thine tekke *on the Judgment Day.*
Thus have I parted company with those who distinguish
between I and thee.(2)

***

Heed thou the Prophet, believer or unbeliever, do him no
injury.
God is offended by cruelty, that no man may injure a heart
with impunity.
As God is my witness, the pit is prepared for such as pay
no mind,
And thus what the scholars have made mine, I have made
thine.(3)

***

When I was one, the spirits came instructing me,
When two, the prophets came and beheld me,
When three, the forty hidden saints came asking, after me
And therefore I entered beneath the ground at sixty-three.(4)

***

O Lord, I have said wisdom is by praise of thee.
Exalted master, seeking refuge I came unto thee.
Repenting, I turned in fear from sin to thee.
Exalted master, seeking refuge I came unto thee.(5)

***

When I was forty-four, in the market of love
I walked distraught and weeping in thine rose garden.
Like Mansur I gave my life on the gallows of love.
Exalted master, seeking refuge I came unto thee.(6)

***

'Tis the destiny given to saints like Mustafa to dwell far from
home.

50

The Yesevis

To the thirty-three thousand Companions and their friends,
To Abu Bakir, 'Umar, 'Uthman and Murtada ['Ali],
Was given the destiny to dwell far from home, So said I.(7)

***

If worship is inspired by aught but by what the eye of the
heart dost see,
Its currency is naught in the tekke.
I have learned these words well,
Thus have I taken lessons from God in eternity.

The station of love is strange, intellect alone will not suffice
thee.
Filled with difficulty and suffering, its affliction never endeth.
And if there are accusations and betrayals they will pass not
away,
Thus have I taken lessons from God in eternity.

If the affliction of love befalleth one, its pang is woe.
It astoundeth, and overwhelms with wonder.
When the eye of the heart opens, love bringeth sorrow,
Thus have I taken lessons from God in eternity.

Wander the deserts, grow thou weary of men and seek thou
love.
If God's creature thou be, then walk thou weeping in fear
of Him.
If thou desirest His countenance, be thou prepared.
Thus have I taken lessons from God in eternity.

Hear ye friends, loves affliction has no remedy.
So long as a heart still beats, love's book is incomplete.
And bones in narrow tombs that lie must there await the
Judgment Day,
Thus have I taken lessons from God in eternity.

Love is a prince, the lover is a pauper, he canst not breathe.
Save by the leave of God, he canst not speak.
Having heard God's word all the world becomes naught but
vanity,
Thus have I taken lessons from God in eternity.(8)

***

The Major Tariqats

If e'er a slave I see, let me be his servant, his slave.
Like the earth o'er his path, the ground beneath his feet,
and I

Consumed by love's flame, extinguished there in ashes lie.
And greeting thus life's end, I passed beneath the ground,
an intimate, a friend.(9)

***

Become thou neither ascetic nor servant, but a lover.
In gratitude hold thou fast to love's path.
Mortify thine flesh, become worthy of thine tekke.
For whosoever hath not love hath neither soul nor faith.(10)

Know thou that humanity means adversity.
The beast maketh the loveless heart his lair.
Weep then if thine heart hath not love.
My pure love poureth out upon him who weeps.

Whosoever love's touch hath felt
Knoweth that fire wherein the "I" doth melt.
God knoweth not but that love is felt.
Maketh thou not then but lovers Lord.

I've made love's sorrow my heart's desire, pain without
remedy.

Where'er love be ne'er disappointed he
Who layeth down his life on her pyre.
Maketh thou naught then but lovers Lord.(11)

***

To whomsoever knoweth not love's flame,
"God's Envoy" is naught but a name.
Tenantless, the refrain upon deaf ears falls,
And truth naught, but confusion calls.(12)

***

Without a sufi guide, neither have they hope.
Without serving, none may in God's grace abide.
They have never wept their nights away,
And none but the tearful countenance attracts God's eye.(13)

***

Prince of eighteen thousand worlds is he, Muhammad.
Guide to thirty-three thousand Companions he, Muhammad.
Contented with hunger and nakedness he, Muhammad.
Intercessor for his rebellious and murderous community,
Muhammad.

Through sleepless nights the Koran recites, Muhammad.
Treating orphans and the needy with generosity, Muhammad.
He guideth those who from the way have strayed,
Muhammad.
Whate'er the need, sufficient is he, Muhammad.

He met Abu Jahil and Bu Lahab with death, Muhammad.
And with censure cleanseth and deliverance bringeth,
Muhammad.
Performer of prayers and fasts, for worship born,
Muhammad.
Glorifier of God, mortifier of flesh, Muhammad.

Resolute guide along the path is he, Muhammad.
Model of the truth and answer be, Muhammad.
Acceptable his prayers, to requests accedes, Muhammad.
Who giveth good for evil, gracious he, Muhammad.

Market place and throne of God and the Highest Heaven
he, Muhammad.
Possessed of eight heavens and sanctity, Muhammad.
'Tis He who maketh wretched Ahmad write, Muhammad.
Possessed of boundless generosity, orphan steeped in poverty,
Muhammad.(14)

The poetry of the *Diwan-i hikmat* remains our primary contact with Ahmad Yesevi and with the early beliefs of the *tariqat* which he founded. These poems unfortunately give us no information about Ahmad Yesevi's *tariqat*. For this we must turn to the *Jawahir al-abrar* (The Jewels of the Upright Ones), a work written by a Yesevi dervish named Khazini. According to this work the Yesevis laid special stress on the importance of the unity of God, the *shari'at* and the *sunnat*, as well as asceticism, solitary contemplation, and *dhikr*.

According to Khazini, a thirteenth century dervish, a *murid* in the Yesevi *tariqat* was expected to do the following:

    1. Unquestioningly obey his murshid *and no one other than his* murshid,

The Major Tariqats

2. *Strive at all times to be alert and to sharpen his intellect,*
3. *Strive to the best of his ability to serve and help his* murshid,
4. *Be true to his word,*
5. *Use his material possessions in the service of his* murshid,
6. *Keep the secrets of the* murshid *and the* tariqat, *and*
7. *Be ever ready to lay down his life on the path mapped out by the* murshid. *(15)*

All members of the *tariqat* were expected to:

1. *Know God fully,*
2. *Practice complete and perfect generosity,*
3. *Practice complete and perfect honesty,*
4. *Strive to perfect their faith through inner enlightenment,*
5. *Make with whatever sustenance may come their way by God's grace, and*
6. *Strive to think deeply and subtly.(16)*

Each Yesevi was also expected to:

1. *Perform the* salat *together with the other members of his* tekke,
2. *Endeavor to be wide awake in the hours just before dawn,*
3. *Think of himself as being at all times in the presence of God,*
4. *Be at all times in a state of ritual purity,*
5. *Strive never to let God be absent from his thoughts, and*
6. *Bow before those dervishes who are* murshids, *wherever he encounters them.(17)*

The Yesevi *tariqat* had a number of characteristic *dhikrs*. The most noted of these is called the *dhikr of the saw*, because of the sawing sound produced in the throat by those performing it.

Performance of this *dhikr* was described by Sheikh Muhammad Ghaws as follows:

Placing both hands on the thighs, and expelling the breath downward toward the navel, the sound 'ha' is articulated (the 'a' sound being drawn out). Then, drawing the breath up from beneath the navel, and holding the body erect, the sound 'hay' is pronounced (this 'hay' being elongated and harsh). In this way, the dhikr *continues. The desired result is obtained by sawing at the heart as a carpenter saws wood....(18)*

It has been reported that some of Yesevi dervishes are still to be found in parts of Turkistan. Elsewhere in the Islamic world the *tariqat* is no longer in existence. On the eve of the rise of the major *tariqats* of Anatolia and the

Balkans, however, it was very much alive. Many Yesevi dervishes left Khorasan and settled in Anatolia where they exerted great influence over the people there. Haji Bektash was the most influential of these dervishes. Before turning our attention to the *tariqat* which he founded, however, it is worth examining the prior birth of another sufi institution which also conditioned the development of *tariqat* life in Anatolia and the Balkans.

Chapter Eight

Futuwwat and the Akhis

Every study of the *tariqats* of Anatolia and the Balkans should include a discussion of *futuwwat* and *akhi* brotherhoods, as these associations, like the *tariqats*, were institutional embodiments of ideas and values developed by sufis. The *akhi* brotherhoods preceded the *tariqats* in Anatolia and the Balkans, and played an important role in the social, economic, and spiritual lives of the Turks living there.

The idea of *futuwwat* can be traced back into early sufism. *Futuwwat* was a word used to denote moral qualities which every Muslim should strive to cultivate: greateartedness, magnanimity, and faithfulness. The Koran describes the Seven Sleepers as exemplifying *futuwwat* (XVIII, 10), though the Prophet's son-in-law, 'Ali, has long been regarded by sufis as its most outstanding exemplar.

Ithar, which means "altruism" or "putting the interests of others ahead of one's own interests," is what lies at the heart of *futuwwat*. (1) *Ithar* appears in the Koran in a verse which praises the behavior of the Prophet's Companions during the Hagira.(2)

Ibn al-'Arabi viewed a *fata* (person possessed of *futuwwat*) as someone who not only puts the interest of others above his own, but who puts faithful obedience to God above obedience to his own desires. He saw this idea reflected in the following Koranic verse:

> *God hath purchased from believers their lives and wealth in order to grant them in return eternal life: they shall fight in the way of Allah and shall slay and be slain.(3)*

He cited the prophet Abraham, who "cast himself into the fire choosing to exalt the Unity of God though it meant agony to his flesh", as an example of this sort of obedience.(4)

According to Ibn al-'Arabi, the generosity and faithfulness which lie at the heart of *futuwwat* are to be seen as signs of power. Meanness and selfishness are, conversely, to be regarded as signs of weakness. God manifests His power in His endless generosity to all men, even those who are His greatest enemies. He feeds them and overwhelms them with His blessing.

Finally, Ibn al-'Arabi sees a connection between *malamat* (reproach) and *futuwwat*. He who strives to be a possessor of *futuwwat* must be willing to suffer the derision and scorn of the many people who view generosity and self-sacrifice as folly.(5)

The word *futuwwat* is also used to refer to a loosely-knit group of brotherhoods which came into being as early as the eighth century. In the thirteenth century the caliph, al-Nasir, tried to bring these brotherhoods under his control. This same caliph sent his adviser, Shihab al-Din 'Umar al-Suhrawardi, to Anatolia in order that he might persuade the ruler of that area, the Seljuk Sultan Kay-Kavus, to foster *futuwwat* brotherhoods there. Although we do not know how Kay- Kavus himself responded to this proposal, we do know that after this time these groups became widespread in Anatolia.(6)

The *futuwwat* brotherhoods which appeared in Anatolia in the thirteenth century were known as *akhi* groups. *Akhi* is a Turkish word which has the same meaning as the Arabic word *fata*: someone who possesses *futuwwat*. It appears that the Anatolian *akhis* took their name from a branch of the *futuwwat* movement which developed in the Turkish provinces of Persia in the eleventh century, though it is not known precisely how the Anatolian *akhis* were influenced by their Persian brethren.

Akhi groups were made up mostly of craftsmen; one of the functions they performed was that of a trade guild. Neşet Çağatay praised the *akhi* groups for finding employment for the great number of craftsmen who flocked to Anatolia from the cities of Asia, for protecting the quality of craftsmanship, for helping the Turkish populace become economically independent, for helping the poor and indigent, and for providing men for the armies of the sultans.(7)

The *akhis* greatly influenced the development of commercial life in Anatolia. They formulated rules and regulations for more than thirty crafts and helped instill a sense of ethics in those who practiced these crafts. The monopoly known as a *gedik* was developed as a result of *akhi* influence. A *gedik*, granted by the state, gave its possessor the exclusive right to carry on a particular trade in a particular area. The *akhis* also fostered the establishment of societies of mutual assistance. Such societies was known as an *esnaf vakfs*. These societies established funds from which *akhis* could obtain loans at an interest rate of one percent. The interest on these loans was set aside by the society to be used for charitable purposes.

Some fascinating light is shed on the *akhis* in Anatolia between 1330 and 1340, by the chronicles of the traveler, Ibn Battutah. It is clear that by this time *akhi* associations had spread throughout the towns of Anatolia. In fact, taking advantage of their famous hospitality, Ibn Battutah most often lodged in one of the lodges.

In Anatolian villages he found groups which called themselves "Associations of Friends".(8) These were the rural equivalent of the *akhi* associations found in the towns. They were active at the end of the harvest season and during the winter months when outdoor activity was restricted to a minimum. Those men of the village who fell between the ages of twenty and forty were eligible for membership. Each of these Associations of Friends was headed by a man known as the *Yaran Başı* (Head of the Friends). He was assisted by an administrative officer, called the *Oda Başı*. The members of these associations were expected to live their lives in accordance with a set of high ethical standards. Those who violated these standards were subjected to

The Major Tariqats

punishments which ranged from being required to take a gift to the person whom they had wronged to being held under freezing cold water. If the violation was quite serious, the offender would be tried in a court over which the *Yaran Başı* presided.

The members of these Associations of Friends were expected to undertake various good works. This could mean helping either an individual or a group. They often served the communities in which they lived by doing things such as building roads or cleaning wells and irrigation canals. Many of the public works of Anatolia were either constructed or repaired by the *akhis*. They aided travelers by putting them up in their communal houses. In the chaotic period which followed the Mongol conquest of Anatolia, the *akhis* prevented anarchy in many towns by managing the affairs of the government themselves.(9)

One of the important activities conducted in the communal houses of the *akhis* was the study of the *futuwwatnamas* (works written to expound the idea of *futuwwat*). This study gave a religious depth to the moral ideals which the *akhis* strove to uphold. The study of *futuwwat* was an essential part of the training given to those who aspired to become members of an *akhi* group.

One of the best known and most venerated leaders of the *akhis* was Akhi Evren (d.659/1261). This veneration extended even to the members of Akhi Evren's family. After his death various of his descendants were successively accorded great authority in the *akhi* organization. Akhi Evren's real name was Sheikh Nasiruddin Abul Haqaik Muhammad b. Ahmad al-Hoyi. He was born in 566/1171 and received his sufi education and training from Ahmad Yesevi's disciples in Khorasan and Transoxiana. It seems that in the course of his travels he met the Turkish sufi Awhaduddin Kirmani and came to Anatolia on his advice. He is traditionally regarded as the founder of the tanner's craft in Anatolia.

A number of pamphlets and some ten longer works have been attributed to Akhi Evren. He is also said to be the author of a collection of letters addressed to Sadruddin Qonawi (d.673/1274), the well-known follower of Ibn al-'Arabi who lived in Konya. From these writings it is evident that although Akhi Evren respected the Twelve Imams of Shi'ite Islam, he was fundamentally a Sunni. In this respect Akhi Evren typifies the early *akhi* movement as a whole, a movement whose members, however much they respected certain tenets of Shi'ism, remained within the fold of Sunni Islam.

Chapter Nine

The Bektashis

The Bektashi *tariqat*, the largest and most influential of all the *tariqats* of Anatolia and the Balkans, was founded by a man known as Haji Bektash (d. 699/1270). Evidence suggests that he was a Yesevi dervish who came to Anatolia from Khorasan. His emigration, like that of Mawlana Jalaluddin Rumi, was probably precipitated by the Mongol invasions. Relatively little is known about his life. We do not know whether his parents were Arabs or Turks. We do know that he was educated in Khorasan. It seems likely that he became a Yesevi dervish at some point in his youth. He arrived in Anatolia when he was about forty years old. Soon after his arrival he may have gotten to know some of the leaders of the Babais, the followers of several *murshids* who were known as *babas* (fathers). These *murshids* were probably Yesevis; their followers were mostly Turcomans, that is to say, Turkish tribesmen. They functioned as both religious and political leaders for the Turcomans whose distinctive religious beliefs and restless, nomadic ways made them unpopular with the Seljuks who ruled Anatolia. The Turcomans, for their part, chafed under this Seljuk overlordship. It thus happened that, led by one of their *babas*, the Turcomans revolted in 1239 or 1240. Haji Bektash was not involved in this revolt, which was eventually quelled by the Seljuks. It seems likely, however, that many of the Babais eventually became his followers.

Haji Bektash settled in Sulucakaraöyük, a place near Kırşehir. It was a remote place, far removed from the centers of Anatolian political and commercial activity. In view of the political strife which was besetting Anatolia at this time, it is quite likely that Haji Bektash chose Sulucakaraöyük because of its remoteness. His choice might also have been influenced by the fact that no *tekkes* existed in Sulucakaraöyük at that time. In any event, after he had established himself there, his fame as a spiritual leader began to spread, and he acquired a considerable following, especially among the Turcomans.

A careful examination of the ideas contained in Haji Bektash's major work, the *Maqalat* (Sayings), reveals that he was essentially a Sunni. Throughout this book he repeatedly emphasizes the importance of following the precepts set forth in the *shari'at*. At one point he says:

> *What exists in the world, what is permissible and forbidden, clean and unclean, is known by means of the shari'at.(1)*

When he writes of the first four caliphs, he likens them to the fingers of a human hand with Muhammad being the thumb; Abu Bakr, the index finger; 'Umar, the middle finger; 'Uthman, the ring finger; and 'Ali, the little finger. A Shi'ite would not have made this comparison, which accords 'Ali a status inferior to that of Abu Bakr, 'Umar and 'Uthman.

The Major Tariqats

According to Coşan the idea that Haji Bektash was a Shi'ite stems from the following lines found in the introduction of one copy of the *Maqalat*:

And confess thou the Twelve Imams.
Reject thou those who oppose them.
Be affectionate to those who are friends to them and show
thou enmity to their detractors
If thou desireth that thine faith be enlightened.

The introductions of other manuscript copies of the *Maqalat* do not, however, contain these lines. Instead, they contain verses lauding Abu Bakr, 'Umar, 'Uthman, and 'Ali. Similarly, no pro-Shi'ite ideas are expressed in the main body of any of the *Maqalat* manuscripts. These facts lead one to conclude that the pro-Shi'ite lines quoted above are not the work of Haji Bektash, but of the person who made that copy of the *Maqalat* in which they appear. This conclusion is given weight by the fact that Hatiboğlu, the writer of the introduction, was a well-known Sunni teacher. It is thus unlikely that he would have been a promulgator of Shi'ite sentiments.(2)

The following excerpts from the *Maqalat* should provide the reader with an idea of its contents:

The heart is the window onto the Padishah of the worlds. Between God and all things there is a veil, but between God and the heart there is none. The heart is like the ka'bah. *The person who would visit the* ka'bah, *who would go there on foot and by the heart, should walk in prostration. It is for this reason that lovers prostrate themselves, faces touching the ground. Those who visit the* ka'bah *need a guide. The Koran is their traveling companion. But the traveling companion of those who journey there by means of the heart is God.*

What is called love is but God's divine kindling and the fireplace of this kindling is the heart of the enlightened.(3)

The heart is an immense city and all that God has created, from the Throne of God to the bottom of the world, exists in that city. The city encompasses all.(4)

The counterpart in man of paradise is the heart.(5)

The city of the heart is ruled by two sultans, one divine and one satanic. The divine sultan is the intellect. The regent of the intellect is religion and its superintendent is submission.(6)

Religion is superior to the intellect.... It is a treasury; intellect is the treasurer. When the treasurer leaves his post, what will the thief do to the treasury? Religion is the sheep; intellect is the shepherd. When the shepherd departs, what will the wolf do to the sheep? Religion is milk; the intellect is the watchman, and the devil is a cur. If the watchman leaves the house and the milk remains unguarded, what will the cur do to the milk?(7)

The intellect is God's balance in the world. There is nothing better in the world than these scales, for it is the intellect which knows and commands every good thing.(8)

The first office of the shari'at *is religion, and the second is knowledge. The third consists of prayer, alms-giving, fasting, and the* hajj—*[the four pillars of the Islamic faith] if means permit.(9) [Note: The fact that he ranks knowledge before the pillars of the faith is a departure from tradition.]*
God has given whatever He has created to man. 'The stars are your mantle, the earth your mattress, the sun and moon your lamps, the fruits your blessing... paradise your destination, the houris *your mates, Ridvan your doorkeeper, the angels your protectors, the* ka'bah *[the cube-like building at the center of the Mosque in Mecca containing the black stone] your* qiblah *[the direction of Mecca toward which all Muslims must turn in prayer], the Koran your belief... Muhammad Mustafa your intercessor, Adam your ancestor, Eve your mother.... You are brothers one to another. I have placed all manner of things at your disposal. From the Throne of God to the bottom of the earth, I have made all things known to you.... Therefore, if you want me, wanting me you will find me. For I am closer to you than the soul to your flesh. I am closer to you than the seeing of your eyes, the speaking of your tongue, or the hearing of your ears. I am closer to you even than your hand's grasp or the walking of your feet. Whatever you know by this knowledge is what you know of yourself. And whoever knows himself knows Me.... There is nothing closer to Adam than the soul and nothing closer to God than man. The soul is close to the flesh, and God is close to man.'(10)*

The head of a man is like the Throne of God. In this world there is sky and earth. Man's back is like the sky and the sole of his foot is like the earth.... The intellect resembles the moon, spiritual knowledge the sun, and intellectual knowledge the stars.... There are seven heavens, and the flesh of man also is in seven layers: the skin, the flesh, the blood, the veins, the nerves.... In the world there are clouds and rain. For a man, worry is like the clouds and tears like the rain....(11)

Haji Bektash's comments on the subject of cleanliness are of interest. He tells us that a Muslim who conforms to the *shari'at* ritually washes himself with water prior to performing the *salat*, as water is the substance which is

The Major Tariqats

best suited to cleanse the human body. He adds, however, that water is unable to purify him who has attained to a true knowledge of God, for such a man knows that he can not be truly cleansed by anything apart from the power of God.

In the *Maqalat*, Haji Bektash speaks of four gates through which a *murid* must pass in order to find God. The first of these is the *shari'at*. The man who has reached this gate is known as an *'abid* (worshipper). The second gate is the *tariqat*. He who has reached this gate is called a *zahid* (ascetic). The third gate is *ma'rifat* (gnosis). The man who has attained this stage is known as an *'arif* (possessor of gnosis). The last gate is *haqiqat* (reality). The *murid* who has reached it is styled *muhib* (lover). At each gate, the *murid* is confronted with ten *maqams* (stations), the obligations of which he must fulfill before he can pass on to the next gate.

Each of these gates represents a stage in a *murid's* spiritual development. In the first stage his primary concern is to follow the dictates of the *shari'at*. In so doing he is in effect worshipping God. He does not yet know God, but he does recognize God's supremacy and expresses this recognition through worship. In the second stage, the *murid* seeks to draw close to God by drawing away from the world. To do this he must practice asceticism. In the third stage the *murid* seeks to attain spiritual knowledge or gnosis. He learns to disregard superficialities that he may penetrate to what lies at the heart of men and events. In the fourth and final stage the *murid* attains to a knowledge of the truth. He truly draws near to God and in doing so becomes enlightened. He learns to be humble. He also learns to divest himself of jealousy and enmity.

The following passages from the *Sharh-i basmalah* (Commentary on the formula, 'In the name of God'), also written by Haji Bektash, speak of prayer, God's Mercy, and His Compassion:

> *Hear me, all who are fearful! Say, 'The Merciful,' that I may make you safe from what you fear. Hear me, all who harbor hope! Say, 'The Compassionate', that your hopes may be realized. Hear me, lovers! Say, 'Allah', so as to escape that ill that your enemies would visit upon you and so as to become friends.(12)*

> *The Exalted One says, 'If a slave has a powerful enemy or if his strength is insufficient, what will he do? He will go and attach himself to an exalted person under whose protection he will be safe from his enemy. Hear me, men! You have an unseen enemy. His name (May he be stoned!) is Satan. Again, you have an unseen Friend: the Merciful and the Compassionate. Therefore recite the* basmalah *[the formula "in the name of God"] that Satan may be driven forth and overcome.'(13)*

> *God said to his Ambassador, 'Hear me, Muhammad! I have gathered together everything in the Four Books which came down from heaven and put it in the* fatihah *[opening* surah *of the Koran]. Whatever*

The Bektashis

there is in the fatihah *I have put in the* basmalah. *If one of your community says, "In the Name of God, the Merciful, the Compassionate", I will count it a merit equal to the recitation by a true believer of all of the Torah, the Gospels, the Psalms and the Koran. What a kindness! What generosity! In exchange for a few polluted drops of water I will bestow such favors and kindness....I have decorated the court of the Book with Compassion, Kindness, and Assistance. It is certain that My gifts will be such as are becoming to My court.'(14)*

In the *Maqalat,* Haji Bektash has this to say about *ghaza* (holy war):

If you kill the unbeliever you are a ghazi *[one engaged in holy war], and if he kills you, you will be a* shahid *[martyr for Islam]... and the rank of martyrs is superior in five respects to that of the prophets. Firstly, the bodies of the prophets were bathed when they died; but those of the martyrs were not. Secondly, the clothes of the prophets were removed when they died, but those of the martyrs were not. Thirdly, the bodies of the prophets were wrapped in shrouds, but those of the martyrs were not. Fourthly, the prophets choose those for whom they will intercede, but the martyrs intercede for their race, their tribe, their relatives, their brothers and sisters, and all those who come to them, for it is through the intercession of the martyrs that all these people will enter paradise. Fifthly, they visit the prophets once a year, but they visit the martyrs every day.(15)*

The idea that those who have been martyred for Islam are more exalted than those whom Islam regards as prophets is very unusual. It may, however, have been inspired by the fact that Muhammad has been depicted in Islamic tradition as both a prophet and a martyr.(16)

This exaltation of martyrdom, however, helped Haji Bektash win the hearts of the Turcomans, a people well known for their soldierly virtues and fighting spirit. It must also have helped make Haji Bektash's thought attractive to the Janissaries, a group with whom the Bektashi *tariqat* was to establish close links.

Although it may be claimed that Haji Bektash deliberately exalted the role of the *ghazi* (fighter for Islam) and the *shahid* (martyr for Islam) in order to make his message appealing to the Turcomans, it can not be said that he won their allegiance by deliberately advocating any of their Shi'ite ideas. His writings are proof of this.

The essence of Haji Bektash's thought and spirit is also to be found in the heartfelt poems of Yunus Emre (d. early 14th c.). The spare simplicity of his style intensifies the emotional impact of his thought. He is today the most widely known and the best-loved of the Turkish sufi poets. Mawlana Jalaluddin Rumi is said to have paid this tribute to Yunus Emre:

Whenever I have scaled the spiritual heights, I have always discovered

The Major Tariqats

that this Turcoman dervish Yunus has been there before me.(17)

All of the following poems are by Yunus Emre:

I am the kingfisher of love, admired of the sea.
The sea is but a droplet within me, its atoms an overflowing
infinity.
The earth is a drop in the sea of space, the sun and moon bow
down to me
The Koran is my guide to eternity, my resting-place and
destiny.(18)

***

What now this sorrow and separation to one in the Friend's
embrace.
Whosoe'er His presence feels, questions not whether He is far
or near,
And if thou wouldst a pilgrim be, turn away from this carrion
place,
And whosoe'er his soul wouldst tend, consider now thine
journey's end.(19)

***

How wondrous this gift of God, this heart which time transforms,
One moment awash in delight, the next steeped in woe,
Of a sudden struck dumb, all words of meaning shorn,
Till suddenly silver tongued, a salve for troubled souls.

One moment plying the starry heights, then plummeting broken
winged,
Now a mere droplet, now a vast ocean bursting its brinks,
Now in a mosque with face pressed down in prayer,
Now in a monastery where with monks the Gospel shares.(20)

***

Science illuminates as it hides,
Truth like glass vanishes before the eye,
And what sense this world in which man lives and dies,
'Tis in the accounting of the next that its meaning lies.

'Tis in the weave of thine self that truth's pattern lies,
Amid the shadows of books the self flits and hides,
Scholars like shades blind eyed by lamp light,
The plague of doubt while all about the cure within them lies.

And how often while with pious works preoccupied,
Did God in his 'khirka' pass wraith-like by,
'Tis worth far more than all thine pious opacity
To enter once through the heart's gate to eternity.(21)

***

No man mayst injure a heart, then pay the price in prayer,
Nor piety nor all humanity canst wash the sin away.
Hold thou fast to the path that hast been prepared for thee,
And if thou wouldst a sufi be, seek thou God with humility.

If thou hast cleaved to the way, to a sufi friend hold fast,
And every good deed will be multiplied a thousand times for thee,
While Yunus with words doth toil, words mixed like honey with
oil,
Words tendered to souls, precious pearls proffered the shoals of
all humanity.(22)

***

No equal hath thee, my God, my destiny!
Let Compassion's flood with forgiveness flow,
That all souls of sin washed clean may rise,
Feather winged on Burak to paradise.(23)

***

I have found the light of life, come looters of my soul,
Plunderers of worldly wares welcome, rob me of my cares.
Relinquishing duality I have returned to the sovereign of unity,
I have imbibed the wine of adversity, come looters of mine
capacity.

'Tis to the self ravaged by sacrifice that the friend doth come,
The ruins of the heart awash in radiant light, may my world be
plundered,
While Yunus with words doth toil, words mixed like honey with
oil,
Words tendered to souls, precious pearls proffered to the shoals
of all humanity.(24)

***

Haji Bektash appointed a number of his trusted followers to be his
assistants. These men were given the title of *khalifahs*. The *Wilayatnama-i Haji*

The Major Tariqats

Bektash, a collection of anecdotes about Haji Bektash, relates that he had thirty-six thousand *khalifahs*. Although this is doubtless a highly exaggerated figure, it does indicate that the number of his assistants must have been large.

According to the *Wilayatnama*, Haji Bektash's favorite *khalifah* was a man named Jamal Sayyid, whom he charged with expounding his teachings in an area along the Mediterranean coast of Anatolia. Another notable *khalifah* was Saru Ismail, a man who acted for a time as Haji Bektash's secretary. He was later called on to spread the ideas of Haji Bektash in the area around Tavos, a town in southwestern Anatolia. It is said that the first person in this region to become a Bektashi was a Christian priest, and that this same priest's church ultimately became a Bektashi *tekke*.

The *Wilayatnama* tells us that Haji Bektash dictated his final will and testament to Saru Ismail as follows:

> *Today is Thursday and today I shall migrate to the next world. Upon my departure cover the door and leave the room. Turn your gaze in the direction of Çile Mountain, for a man mounted on a grey steed will ride forth from there. A green scarf will cover his face. After he has dismounted and left his horse at my door, he will enter and read to me the* Yasin Surah *of the Koran. When he dismounts and greets you, receive his greeting and entertain him.... He will wash my body. As he washes, pour the water for him; help him....*
>
> *May the son of Fatima Ana [Kadıncık Ana], Hızır Lale, become my successor. He will serve for fifty years. He will be succeeded in turn by his son Mürsel, who will serve for 48 years. His successor will be his son Yusuf Balı, who will serve for thirty years and who will draw near to God. This is the state of the world: those who come shall pass away. Serve thou also. Lay out the meal. If you need help, seek it in generosity. When the people wanted courage and a miracle from Murtada ['Ali], he commanded Kanbar, saying, 'Lay on the meal'. Let all who would enter the tariqat and wear its dress seek out a traveler and serve him. Let them not become as Satan. Let them not provoke others unnecessarily. Let them not puff themselves up before others. Let them not envy....(25)*

Kolu Açık Hajim Sultan was another of Haji Bektash's *khalifahs*. The *Wilayatnama* relates that when Haji Bektash gave Hajim Sultan the sword of the *batin* (sword with the power to cut through surface appearances to mystical meanings) he warned him to avoid all unjust acts lest the sword do him grave injury. In order to test the powers of the sword, however, Hajim Sultan cut a donkey in half, an act which provoked Haji Bektash to curse him, saying, "May his arm be paralyzed!". This curse was realized.

Hajim Sultan is the only Bektashi *khalifah* whose life formed the subject of a collection of anecdotes known as the *Wilayatnama-i Hajim Sultan*. According to this work, Hajim Sultan spread the ideas of Haji Bektash in the area around Susuz, a place near Uşak in western Anatolia. He too is reported to have caused Christians to become Bektashis. The fact that the village in which he lived came to bear his name attests to the regard which the people of this area had for him.

Sarı Saltuq (d.663/1264) was a dervish who is regarded by some as a *khalifah* of Haji Bektash and by others as the founder of *tekkes* which were eventually amalgamated with those established by Haji Bektash and his *khalifahs*. In any event it is clear that Sarı Saltuq was a great spiritual leader. It appears that he was loved and respected by all who knew him, Muslim and Christian alike. Although he worked mostly in Rumeli, we know his fame spread as far as southern Russia, because in 1332 Ibn Battutah, the well-known Arab traveler, heard the Tartars of this area recount legends about Sarı Saltuq.

Haji Bektash is said to have singled out one person among his followers to be his successor as the head of the *tariqat*. The identity of this person is, however, a matter of debate. Some claim that he wished his surviving sons to succeed him, each in turn, beginning with the eldest and ending with the youngest. Others claim that he appointed someone outside his family to succeed him. There are those who claim that the ties between Haji Bektash and his so-called sons were not consanguineal, but spiritual, since a *murshid* is traditionally regarded as a *murid's* spiritual father. The Ottoman chronicler, Aşıkpaşazade, claimed that he designated a woman known as Kadıncık Ana as his successor. This, however, would have been highly unlikely.

Kadıncık Ana is, however, an intriguing figure in Bektashi history. She was a woman of Sulucakaraöyük, the village which Haji Bektash made his headquarters. Her deep interest in sufism soon caused her to become one of Haji Bektash's most devoted followers. One group of Bektashis, whom we shall call the adherents of the Çelebi, believe that she eventually became his wife and bore him three sons. As they believe that Haji Bektash wished his sons to succeed him as leader of the *tariqat*, they decided that the leadership of the *tariqat* belongs to someone who can show that he is a descendant of Haji Bektash through one of these sons. To this person they give the title of *Çelebi*. Another group, whom we shall refer to as the adherents of the *Dede* (grandfather), do not believe that Haji Bektash married or fathered children. For them there is thus no question of a succession based on blood. They prefer to bestow the leadership upon whomever their leaders deem worthy of it. The person whom they choose is given the tile of *Dede*. Thus the *tariqat* was effectively split into two groups, each with its own head. The *Dede's* adherents were most numerous in the towns and cities, whereas the *Çelebi's* adherents were more likely to be found in villages in Anatolia.

Over the long span of time which has elapsed since the death of Haji Bektash in 1270, Bektashi thought has been most noticeably influenced by two men: Fadlullah Hurufi (d. 796/1393) and Balım Sultan (d. 922/1516).

Fadlullah Hurufi was born in Khorasan and appears to have spent all of his life in Iran. He set forth his ideas in various works of prose and verse, the most famous of these being the *Javidannama* (The Book of Eternity).

The Major Tariqats

Fadlullah claimed that he was an incarnation of the Divine and that he had been sent into the world to give man a more complete revelation of God's will. According to one of Fadlullah's doctrines, this more complete revelation could be obtained by learning to read God's previous revelations in a new way. To do this one needed to learn the hidden meaning of each of the letters in all the alphabets in which God's revelations had been written. One could then use these meanings to find the true message hidden within each of these divine texts. Fadlullah knew what these hidden meanings were, and he regarded it as his mission to impart this knowledge to man. As he viewed the Koran as the most complete of all of God's written revelations, he devoted most of his time to teaching his disciples how to interpret it.

Although Fadlullah's claims were heretical, this did not prevent their being attractive to many. He gained a number of followers, some of whom brought his ideas to Anatolia, where they took root among the Bektashis. Fadlullah Hurufi's ideas so influenced the Bektashis that a number of chroniclers came to regard "Bektashi" as a synonym for "Hurufi". The historians Jacob and Hasluck even hazarded the speculation that the true founder of the Bektashi *tariqat* might have been Fadlullah Hurufi.(26) The leading propagandists of the Hurufis in Anatolia were 'Ali A'la (d.822/1419) and the poet Nesimi (d.820/1417). On account of his heretical Hurufi beliefs the latter was cruelly put to death by being flayed alive.

When Balım Sultan (d.922/1516) acceded to the headship of the *tariqat* around 1500, diversity in belief and in worship was prevalent among those who called themselves Bektashis. Balım Sultan sought to make this loosely-knit group into a unified brotherhood. To do this he tried to make certain beliefs and rituals standard throughout the *tariqat*, an endeavour in which he proved markedly successful. The degree of his success can be measured by the fact that the beliefs and practices which are adhered to by the Bektashis of today are essentially those advocated by Balım Sultan.

We must note, however, that the ideas which Balım Sultan promoted were quite different from those of Haji Bektash. Shi'ite beliefs were preeminent in Balım Sultan's thought. He believed, for example, in the doctrine of the Twelve Imams, a belief which his followers began to express symbolically by wearing a *taj*, a round brimless hat, with a crown made up of twelve segments.

This belief was symbolized in other ways as well. During Balım Sultan's time, it was decided that each *tekke* would be governed by a hierarchy of twelve persons, each of whom was to be selected from among the leading members of the *tekke*. A post related to the running of the *tekke* was assigned to each of these persons. Each of these posts was symbolically associated with a historical or legendary figure revered by Bektashis. When ceremonies took place at the *tekke*, these twelve hierarchs sat on sheepskins (*posts*) placed at regular intervals around the perimeter of the *maydan*, the open area in the center of the main room of a *tekke*. These twelve *posts*, together with the names of the personages associated with them, are as follows:

Illustration 15

BABAYI.

Illustration 16

Illustration 17   DERWISCH BEKTASCHY.   71

SCHEÏKH des BEKTASCHYS.

Illustration 18

Illustration 19 BEKTASCHY *VOYAGEUR*.

Illustration 20

74

Illustration 21

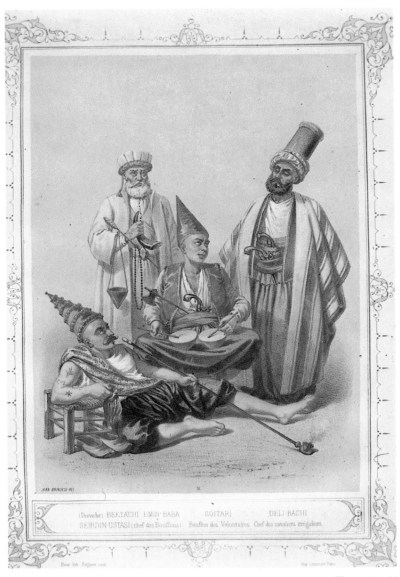

(Dervche) BEKTACHI EMIN-BABA   SOITARI   DELI-BACHI
SEIRDIN-USTASI (chef des Bouffons)   Bouffon des Volontaires. Chef des cavaliers irréguliers.

Illustration 22

76

1. Sheikh—Haji Bektash

2. Cook—Sayyid 'Ali Sultan

3. Baker—Balım Sultan

4. Warden or Registrar—Kaygusuz Sultan

5. Groom—Kamber 'Ali

6. Keeper of the Maydan—Saru Ismail

7. Keeper of the Tomb—Kara Donlu Can Baba

8. Keeper of the Larder—Şahkulu Hajim Sultan

9. Coffee Maker—Shah Shadhali Sultan

10. Sacrificer—the Prophet Abraham

11. Keeper of the Shoes—Abdal Musa Sultan

12. Keeper of the Guesthouse—the Prophet Khizir

There were also twelve tasks carried out by various members of a Bektashi *tekke* in connection with the ceremony known as the *Ayin-i jam'*. Bektashis associated each of these tasks with someone who was close to 'Ali, because 'Ali himself was supposed to have assigned these tasks to his sons, friends, and relatives at various times. These tasks, together with the names of the historical personages associated with them, are as follows:

1. Organizing the *tariqat*—Imam Hasan

2. Sweeping—Imam Husayn

3. Barbering—Mehmed Hanafi

4. Chanting—'Abdussamad

5. Setting the table—'Abdulwahid

6. Pouring water for Ablutions—Salmani

7. Pouring Water or Wine—Tayyib

The Major Tariqats

8. Being a factotum—'Abdulmu'in

9. Being a Watchman—'Abdulkarim

10. Being a Herald—'Abdullah

11. Lighting Candles and Wicks—Hadi Akbar

12. Being the Doorman—'Abduljalil

After Balım Sultan, Bektashis came to hold many ideas which ran counter to the beliefs of most Muslims, Sunnites and Shi'ites alike. Most of these were probably promoted by Balım Sultan. Bektashis came to believe, for example, that Allah, the Prophet, and 'Ali, were all three united in one godhead. They formed, in other words, a trinity. They also came to believe that after death a human soul could be reincarnated in human or animal form. Balım Sultan apparently taught that those Bektashis who had passed through the gates of *ma'rifat* and *haqiqat* should be allowed to drink wine. This toleration of something which most Muslims regard as forbidden is but one example of what appears to have been a general disregard for outward form on the part of Balım Sultan. Many Bektashis took this disregard to heart and soon Bektashis as a group became noted for such things as not heeding the call to prayer or not observing the fast during the month of Ramadan. This disregard for the outward forms of religion appears to have increased with the passage of time. We find, for example, that it eventually became customary for all Bektashis to drink alcoholic beverages.

Another controversial idea which can be traced back to Balım Sultan is the belief that the practice of celibacy could help one draw closer to God. His supporters are known to have countered the *hadith* which forbids celibacy with the contention that marriage, according to the *sunnat*, is a *fard-i kifayah*, namely a duty which, if carried out by some, is not binding upon all. Celibacy was not, however, made obligatory for Bektashis. On the contrary, it was an option which was open only to those who, by passing through the gate of *haqiqat*, had gained the title of *dervish*. The only Bektashi who was required to be celibate was the man who was chosen to be the *Dede*, the head of that branch of the Bektashi *tariqat* whose members did not believe that the headship had been vouchsafed exclusively to those who were supposedly blood descendants of Haji Bektash.

The beliefs and practices promoted by Balım Sultan were not, however, restricted to the adherents of the *Dede*. Most of them were adopted by the adherents of the *Çelebi* as well. If we except the fact that the adherents of the *Çelebi* do not practice celibacy it is safe to say that their beliefs and practices are essentially the same as those of the adherents of the *Dede*.

The adherents of the *Dede* used various terms to describe the spiritual status of those in their branch of the *tariqat*. We have already discussed the terms *'abid, zahid, 'arif*, and *muhib*. In addition to these we find the terms *ashiq, dervish*, and *baba*. An *ashiq* is someone who frequently visits a *tekke* and shows a great interest in the Bektashi way of life, but who has not yet decided to become a Bektashi. A *dervish* is a *muhib* who has decided to forsake secular life completely. *Dervishes* are often celibate and often actually live in a *tekke*. A *baba* is a *dervish* who has become the head of a *tekke*. The *dede* was usually chosen from among the *babas*.

The most important ceremony of the Bektashi *tariqat* is a ritual known as the *Ayin-i jam'*. The ceremony includes the initiation of new members of the *tariqat*, and ends with a communal meal and a dance accompanied by music. As a whole, the ceremony constitutes the communal *dhikr* of the Bektashis. Those *murids* who are undergoing initiation may be either men or women, as the Bektashis, unlike most *tariqats*, allow women to join their ranks. Women are not, however, permitted to advance to positions of leadership within a *tekke*.

The part of the ceremony devoted to the initiation of new members(27) begins with the *murid's* kneeling before his *murshid* and kissing first the knees and chest of the *murshid* and then the floor in front of him. This act of respect and submission is known as the *niyaz* (entreaty). It is an act which the Bektashis regard as symbolizing the prostration of the angels before Adam, an event recounted in the Koran. In the Koranic story, as in the Bektashi *niyaz*, that which is being revered is not man, but the spirit of God dwelling within man.

After performing the *niyaz* the *murid* asks God to pardon his sins. The *murid* then declares his or her intention to live a new life, one in which he or she will avoid "all that is transitory and ephemeral, all worldly desires and preoccupations, and all that prevents man from drawing near to God." Following this the *murid* asks God's blessing on Muhammad. The *murshid* then says the following:

> *Are you prepared to surrender to your* murshid *in the* maydan *of the saints and in the presence of the* Pir *[Founder of the* tariqat, Haji Bektash]? In that case do not do what has been forbidden. Do not lie. Do not commit adultery or enter into homosexual relations. Do not take what does not belong to you. Do not tell all that you see. Do not know all that you know. Do not tell all that you hear.*

These admonitions are followed by this question:

> *Do you believe in the trinity of God, Muhammad, and 'Ali; the Twelve Imams; and the line of the Family of the Prophet?*

After the *murid* has given an affirmative answer to this question, certain verses of the Koran are read. The *murshid* then addresses the *murid* as follows:

> *Have you reconciled yourself to accept all that God may visit upon you? Have you submitted yourself to divinely ordained destiny? Know-*

The Major Tariqats

ing these two to be one, have you, with the help of your murshid, *united the trinity of God, Muhammad, and 'Ali in your heart, day and night? Do you know what we call 'true' to be true, and 'false' to be false? Will you be ashamed before God on the Day of Judgment if you then find you had been deceived by a hypocrite who had only pretended to be a man of God? Do you accept the* ijtihad *[judgment in legal matters] of Jafar Sadiq as being true and do you believe that which we call 'false' is truly false? Do you know who your* rehber *[guide] and* murshid *is? Have you looked upon those whom the Prophet loved as your friends and those whom he did not love as your enemies? If you should retract this confession will you be ashamed on the Day of Judgment? May God, Muhammad, and 'Ali bless you in this confession.*Hu *[He, i.e. God]. (28)*

After having answered all these questions in the affirmative, the *murid* says this:

I am a slave of God. I am of the offspring of Adam. I am of the nation of Abraham. My religion is Islam; my book is the Koran;·my qiblah *is the* ka'bah. *I am of the community of the* najiya *[saved ones] and of the school of Imam Jafar al–Sadiq. God is great; God is great; God is great.*

With this the initiatory part of the ceremony ends. It is followed by a long celebratory meal during which wine is consumed. The *Ayin-i jam'* culminates in a *sama'* (lit. hearing) or dance accompanied by music. The dance is performed by men and women in mixed couples. The couples begin by bending their bodies first to the right and then to the left. These movements, which are executed slowly at first, gradually accelerate. At a designated point in the dance the couples place their left hands on their left breasts, bow, and then begin swinging their arms to the left and right in time with the bending movements of their bodies. After a time the couples begin to move in a circle around the room. Finally they begin to whirl as they circle, at first slowly and then more rapidly as the tempo of the music increases. In this way, movement and music combine with the effects of wine to lift the participants into a state of ecstasy. Enemies of the Bektashis have often described this part of the *Ayin-i jam'* as an orgy of drunkenness and sexual license. Those who have been present at this celebration know such malicious assertions to be unfounded.

The Bektashi *tariqat* was distinguished by the special ties it had with the Janissaries, a crack corps of infantrymen in the Ottoman army. The Janissaries were originally made up of men who had been born into Christian families. These men were taken from their families at a young age, converted to Islam, and trained to serve as soldiers in this corps. They were forbidden to marry. In time these practices fell into disuse, and the corps became made up of married men born of Muslim parents.

The Bektashis

We do not know how these ties between the Bektashis and the Janissaries came into being. Haji Bektash himself had nothing to do with the founding of the Janissaries despite an old tradition which says that he did. It is clear, however, that at some point in its early history a tie was established between this corps and the Bektashi *tariqat*. As a result of this it came about that every Janissary was expected to become a Bektashi. Parallel with this there arose the custom of assigning a *murshid* to every Janissary group. These developments made each of these groups of Janissaries, in effect, a Bektashi fraternity. The following discharge paper(29) given to a Janissary named Mahmud in 1822 is an interesting testimony of this bond between the Janissaries and the Bektashis:

> *I have Trusted in God*
> *Company* (Bölük) 45
>
> *We are believers from of old. We have confessed the unity of Reality. We have offered our head on this Way. We have a prophet, 'Ahmedi Mukhtar Janab'. Since the time of the Heroes (*Erler*) we have been the intoxicated ones. We are the moths in the divine fire. We are a company of wandering dervishes (*serseri divaneler*) in this world. We cannot be counted on the fingers; we cannot be finished by defeat. No one outside of us knows our state. We have affirmed the Twelve Imams, the Twelve Ways, the Three, the Seven, the Forty, the Light of the Prophet, the Beneficence (*Kerem*) of 'Ali, and our Pir, the head sultan, Haji Bektash Wali. In one thousand two hundred and thirty-eight in conformity with the benevolent arrangement established by the Lawgiver, the Conqueror 'Sultan Süleyman Han', whose place is in Paradise and whose abode is Heaven, and by permission of the Ağa of the Soup-Makers (*Çorbacı*), and with the knowledge of all the elders this Discharge Certificate (*Suffa*) has been given to 'Mahmud' who has sought and desired it, and whose name is written in the Record-book of the Way. When required let it be shown.*

(Seal)	*(Seal of)*
I have trusted in God	*'Mehmet'*
Commander (Usta)	*Chief of the Barrack*
'Hüseyin'	*(Odabaşı)*
	12 38"
	45

Their ties with the Janissaries did not, however, work to the good of the Bektashis when the Ottoman sultan decided to suppress this corps in 1826. Long before 1826, however, the Janissary Corps had disintegrated into a mutinous

The Major Tariqats

and unruly Praetorian Guard which, instead of striking terror into the hearts of the sultans' enemies, struck terror into the hearts of the sultans themselves. This situation came to an end in 1826 when Sultan Mahmud II eliminated the Janissaries at one stroke by having his troops kill every Janissary they could find throughout the Ottoman empire. Those of the corps who managed to stay alive had to conceal their identity. Owing to its close association with the Janissary corps the Bektashi *tariqat* suffered suppression as well. Its *tekkes* were confiscated, and its leaders were either executed or exiled. The Sunni religious leaders charged the Bektashis with flagrantly violating various precepts of Islam. The Nakshbandis, an order which was highly Sunnite in its beliefs, were particularly virulent in their attacks. Most of the confiscated Bektashi *tekkes* were turned over to them. Despite these harsh measures the Bektashi *tariqat* did not die. It continued to exist openly in those rural areas which could not be effectively controlled by the central government, and its *tekkes* remained open in many of the towns and cities located in the Balkan domains of the Ottoman Empire. It was only in Istanbul and in the towns and cities of Anatolia that the *tariqat* had to live a clandestine existence.

The Bektashi *tariqat* gained some prominence during the Turkish War of Independence (1918-1923) when Mustafa Kemal Atatürk, the leader of the Turkish Nationalist forces and first president of the Republic of Turkey, sought Bektashi support. He was particularly anxious to gain the support of the *Çelebi's* adherents, as most of them dwelt either in central or in eastern Anatolia, areas the support of which was vital to the Nationalist cause. Atatürk was successful in this effort. The Bektashi *tariqat* rallied to support the Nationalists.

The two men who served as *Çelebi* during these years were enthusiastic in their support of Atatürk. Both of them served as deputies in the Grand National Assembly, the main legislative body of the newly formed Republic of Turkey. The following letter, written by Çelebi Veliyuddin Efendi to his adherents in 1923, is a striking testimony of this support:(30)

> *To all the sincere friends and esteemed descendants of my ancestor Haji Bektash of Anatolia:*
>
> *All of you have heard what has been said by Ghazi Mustafa Kemal Paşa, the man who has restored the nation and secured its independence, the man whose existence is a source of pride for Muslims everywhere, and the man who now serves as the esteemed head of the Grand National Assembly of Turkey.*
> *We should reckon it our duty to realize all of his plans for the progress and upliftment of our nation. His sound ideas will set our nation free and secure our happiness. We will have nothing whatsoever to do with those who deny this. I very strongly urge you to vote only for those candidates recommended to you by the aforementioned Ghazi. By so doing, you will be working for the liberation of the homeland. Those who do not act in accordance with this advice shall no longer be reckoned*

*a part of our number. Men of God shall have nothing to do with them.
Let me state once again that it is Ghazi Mustafa Kemal Paşa alone who
can save this nation. Those who stand by him are the true sons of the
blessed homeland. Do not listen to what anyone else may tell you. Follow
my advice to the letter. The man who heads the Grand National Assembly
is the man who is thinking of your happiness, the man who will free
you from slavery. He is the greatest man among us. His name is Mustafa
Kemal Paşa.*
    March 25, 1339 (1923)

Haji Bektash Wali Çelebi

Having pledged their support to Atatürk and the Republic, how did the
Bektashis react to the law, passed in November 1925, which suppressed all the
tariqats in Turkey? Some responded favorably, saying that there was no longer
any real need for the Bektashi *tariqat* because the Republican government had
realized the social reforms which the Bektashis had always hoped to achieve:
abolition of the caliphate, the liberation of women, and the suppression of
religious fanaticism.(31) This argument was, of course, special pleading: men
did not join the Bektashis primarily because they wished to see these reforms
instituted, as a *tariqat* is not a political party. Most Bektashis were undoubtedly
saddened by the promulgation of this law.

Nevertheless, just as the suppressive measures of 1826 did not do away
with the Bektashi *tariqat* in the Ottoman Empire, so the proscriptive law of
1925 did not put an end to its existence within the Republic of Turkey. After
1925 the Bektashi *tariqat* like the other *tariqats* in Turkey did not suddenly
become extinct. Instead it began to exist as a secret organization. This was
not difficult for its members because it was a rule of the *tariqat* that its members
might not divulge the affairs of the *tariqat* to anyone who was not a Bektashi.
Today the Bektashi *tariqat* numbers roughly three million adherents within
Turkey, and continues to have numerous adherents in the Balkan countries.(32)

No discussion of the Bektashis should omit to mention that among the
tariqats they are distinguished by the fact that they accord women a relative
measure of equality. This is exemplified by their allowing women to become
members of the *tariqat*, as well as by their disapproval of divorce on virtually
any grounds apart from infidelity. If we consider that Haji Bektash was supposed to have been a member of the Yesevis, a group known to have allowed
women to participate in their *dhikrs*, then it is quite possible to infer that it
was he who made these ideas a part of Bektashi thought.

Chapter Ten

The Mawlawis

Mawlana Jalaluddin Rumi (d.672/1273), the founder of the Mawlawi *tariqat*, was born Muhammad Jalaluddin on 30 September 1207 in Balkh, a city in Khorasan. His father, Bahaaddin Walad, was a preacher and teacher, and his paternal grandfather, Husayin, was a well-known scholar. His mother was related to the Khwarizmshahs, the rulers of Khwarizm, an area located just south of the Aral Sea. When Rumi was still a child his family left Balkh in order to escape the army of Genghis Khan, which was advancing towards Khwarizm. They traveled westward and eventually arrived in Anatolia, which was then known as Rum.(1) In 1228 they took up residence in Konya, owing to the fact that Bahaaddin Walad had attained a teaching post there. Upon the latter's death in 1230, this post was given to Rumi, who had studied the Islamic sciences under his father and had been initiated into the sufi way by a *murshid* named Sayyid Burhanaddin Muhaqqiq Tirmidhi.

Rumi's great mystical genius did not become apparent until it was kindled into flame as a result of his friendship with Shams-i Tabrizi,a dervish whom he met in Konya in 1244. Shams-i Tabrizi, also known as Shamsaddin Tabrizi, was a powerful personality possessed of great spiritual gifts. The spiritual bond which developed between them was so intense that Rumi began to neglect his family, friends, and students in order to be with Shams. The two of them are said to have secluded themselves from the world for six months on end in order to meditate and converse. The intensity of Rumi's feeling for Shams, whom he regarded as an inspired bearer of divine love, is apparent in the following excerpts from his writings:

> *Were I east or west, were I to ascend to the heavens, and were I to find no trace of thee, then neither would I have found any trace of eternal life. I was first among ascetics in the land, lord of the lectern; and then an accident of the heart brought me to a love which can do naught before thee but caress thine hands....*
>
> *Once I was in love with books. I towered above other scholars and other men of letters. But upon beholding him whose hands proffered the wine of divine love, I became drunk and broke my pens. I performed my ablution in a rain of tears. The* qiblah *of my worship became the face of the beloved. If any obstacle should come between me and thee, may it be torn asunder. Far better, if I must live bereft of thee, for my existence to be consigned to fire. 'Tis thou who art my lover in the* ka'bah, *and in the church....*
>
> *The flames of love leap beyond the face of the earth and the throne of· God. And in these flames I can not conceal the face of Shamsaddin....*

The Mawlawis

Shams-i Tabriz is the sheikh of religion, the oceanic meaning of the Lord of the Worlds. He is the sea of the soul. He is that rushing and spuming, that flowing and renewing sea. Before him, the earth, the heavens, all existing things, are as nothing....

Though a shadowless sun, Mawlana moves in an orbit around Shams. He has been drawn into his light, drowned in his radiance.... When Shams sunlike rises, all shadows vanish....(2)

Rumi's family and friends, bitterly resenting the fact that Rumi neglected them in order to be with Shams, decided to rectify things by getting rid of Shams. This was accomplished in the first instance by persuading him to go to Syria. Rumi, however, became so distraught by this loss that his family and friends agreed to allow Shams to return to Konya. Upon his return, however, Rumi once again began to neglect his family and friends in order to be with him. Once more they acted to remove Shams from Konya, and this time they were successful in removing him permanently. Whether or not they did this by killing him has remained a matter of debate.

After this loss Rumi devoted the rest of his life to expressing what he had experienced and learned during his time with Shams. One result of this was a truly remarkable literary outpouring in verse. Rumi's poetry, especially his long poem known as the *Mathnawi*, contains some of the most beautiful passages of mystical verse ever written. His greatness as a poet and as a mystic gained him many disciples. As time passed these disciples began to coalesce into a loosely organized *tariqat* headed by Rumi, whom they respectfully referred to as Mawlana (Our Master). Rumi died in 1273, but his spirit has continued to live "in the hearts of those who know God by the heart."(3)

The heart of Rumi's message is that love is the motive force of the universe. Properly understood, the universe is a harmonious whole in which every part is related to all others in a love which finds its common focus in God. Having been created as part of this harmonious whole, indeed as its crown, man can achieve harmony with both himself and the universe only if he learns to love God. His love for God will then lead him to love, not only his fellow man, but all things which God has created. Drawing near to God through love is for Rumi, as for all sufis, the way to true fulfillment in life. What made Rumi famous was his ability to convey this message in poetry of surpassing beauty. He can describe with equal eloquence both the joy of drawing close to God and the sorrow of separation from God. Like other mystical writers he portrays God as the beloved, and the human soul searching for God as the lover.

Rumi is particularly adept at capturing the pathos of man's separation from God. In the verse introduction to the *Mathnawi*, the poetical work for which he is best known, he writes of a reed which has been torn from its reedbed and made into a flute. When played, however, the sound of the flute is not cheerful but sad. It is as if the flute were mourning its separation from the reedbed, the place where it had flourished as a living plant. The reed is a metaphor for man whose home was originally in God prior to his coming into

The Major Tariqats

the world. Separated from God by the world man, like the reed flute, can only sing a song full of yearning and sadness:

> *Listen to the lament of the reed,*
> *To its sad tale of separation,*
> *Crying, 'Ever since from the reedbed born,*
> *My lament hath caused men to mourn.*
>
> *Mine is the voice of sorrow in every land,*
> *The pain of loss in every man.*
> *Mine is the wound that will not heal,*
> *The mysterious pain that all men feel.*
>
> *And I am a flame dancing in love's fire,*
> *That flickering light in the depths of desire.*
> *Wouldst thou know the pain that severance breeds,*
> *Listen then to the strain of the reed. (4)*

Rumi also believed that just as man reaches out to God in love, so God reaches out to man in love. The greatest testimony to God's love for man is, in Rumi's belief, the message of Islam. Rumi unhesitatingly proclaimed this in these words:

> *So long as my soul remains in my body I am a slave of the Koran;*
> *I am soil on the road of Muhammad. If it should come to pass that*
> *my words are interpreted otherwise, I take issue with that interpreta-*
> *tion; I am wearied by it and by him who makes it.(5)*

Rumi nevertheless believed that Muslims were by no means the only people to whom God had revealed himself. He made this clear when he wrote the following:

> *O ye who harbor within thee Gabriels by the thousands,*
> *O ye Messiahs, lowly beast of burden whose lights few com-*
> *prehend,*
> *O ye thousand secret* ka'bahs *in Christian congregation,*
> *'Tis ye who are the spaceless places of prostration.(6)*

Islam represented for Rumi the shortest and easiest path to God. At the same time, however, he believed that all men are on the path to God, for all men at some point come to realize, however dimly, that they are exiles in this world, cut off from that which originally nurtured them and which still remains the ground of their being. Inspired by Junayd al–Baghdadi's conception of the *mithaq* (Primeval Covenant) Rumi believed that all men are bound to spend their lives on earth searching for God. If this is so then those who call themselves unbelievers are searchers who are unconscious of the object of their search; whereas those who know themselves to be believers are the searchers who are conscious of it. The fact that all of these searchers take such varied paths is not a matter of importance to Rumi. What matters to him is that the paths of all men are destined by the Primeval Covenant to end in God.

For Rumi God was not to be found by intellectual means. Love was the way to finding God:

> *Love is the astrolabe of God's secrets. This way or that, love guides all to eternity. Words may enable us to understand, but ineffable love... is the best enlightener. The intellect becomes like a donkey mired in mud in its efforts to explain love. It is love which explains love.... The evidence of the sun is the sun. If you require proof, turn your face from it....(7)*

Inherent in the idea of man's separation from God is the idea of suffering: the uprooted reed sings a song of lamentation. Man, who is essentially a stranger to this world, can not be expected to be gently treated by it. On the contrary, trials and sufferings are his lot. Rumi tells us that "Adam came into the world to weep, to cry out, to moan, to be melancholy."(8) This suffering, however, has a redeeming quality, for through suffering man learns to turn his eyes to God. The man who suffers much comes to see that all is false apart from what is of God. Suffering can thus be seen, according to Rumi, as a sign of God's grace.

> *'Tis by God's grace bestowed,*
> *The blessed pain of grief, of woe.*
> *Glad the tearful eyes that burn for Him,*
> *Happy the mournful heart that yearns for Him.*
> *Laughter is the end of lamentation,*
> *Tears a prelude and preparation.*
> *Where there is greenery water runs,*
> *Where there are tears grace comes.*
> *Like a moaning, groaning waterwheel, weep*
> *For where'er tears flow, there green life grows.(9)*

When man's trial-ridden existence on earth has come to an end, his spirit will return to its home in God. Rumi, using the word "I" to signify man's spiritual self, describes this return in the following verse:

> *'Tis I to senseless matter a self imparted,*
> *And I from dumb matter dying, departed.*
> *'Twas then I, the verdant vigor in the vine,*
> *And I amid the withered leaves who died.*
> *'Twas I, that thrilling surge in bestial veins,*
> *And I who purged by death rose up again.*

The Major Tariqats

'Tis now I the man must die, but the "I" will ever rise,
'Til arm-in-wing with angels, it plies the starry heights.
But higher still than angels' wings can soar,
The "I" will rise up, ever in search of more,
'Til shedding angels' wings, beyond the limits of speech,
It rises vanishing beyond imagination's reach.
And joyous the passage beyond all things,
The eternal release which death finally brings.
For 'tis written that when death intones its final refrain,
All things will pass, only His face will remain.(10)

Another sign of God's grace is the fact that he has sent man guides to aid and comfort him in his exile here on earth. For Rumi the greatest of these guides is the Prophet Muhammad, who although no longer alive continues to be physically represented in the world by his *murshids*. Rumi himself is of course regarded by his followers as a great exemplar of what such a *murshid* should be.

With the exception of the Prophet Muhammad few men of religion have combined in their persons both religious and organizational genius. Rumi was decidedly not of these few. He was not interested in organizing his followers into a *tariqat*. This was the task of his immediate successors: Çelebi Husam (1273-1284), Sultan Walad (1284-1312); and Ulu 'Arif Çelebi (1312-1320). By the time of the death of Ulu 'Arif's son and successor, Shamsaddin Amir 'Alim (d.798/1395), the Mawlawi *tariqat* had spread throughout Anatolia.

We shall now look at the initiation ceremony which the Mawlawis developed. It begins with the *murid's* seating himself cross—legged on the floor before the sheikh of the *tekke*. The sheikh then takes the *murid's* hand and asks him to repent and to promise that he will henceforth devote himself to doing only what is right. After the *murid* has declared himself to be penitent and vowed to change his ways, the sheikh instructs him in the recitation of the *kalima-i tawhid* (the Declaration that God is One) and the Mawlawi *dhikr*. When this has been done the sheikh solemnly cuts a tuft of hair from a spot just above the *murid's* forehead.(11)

Following this the *murid* is ready to be invested with the *taj* (dervish hat) and the *khirka* (dervish cloak). The *murid* kneels before the sheikh laying his head upon the sheikh's knees. The sheikh or his assistant then recites the Mawlawi *silsilah* (chain of spiritual succession). When this recitation has ended the sheikh bids the *murid* to put on the hat and the cloak. The *fatihah* is then recited. After this the *murid* kisses the hands of all the dervishes of higher rank.

According to the Turkish scholar Abdülbaki Gölpınarlı the Mawlawis would occasionally perform a *dhikr* in the following way:

The sheikh would sit on a red animal hide spread out in front of the mihrab. *His back would be facing the* mihrab. *The* dedes *[dervishes of higher rank]*, dervishes, *and* muhibs *[dervishes of lower rank] would kneel in a circle in front of the sheikh. The dervish kneeling immediately opposite the sheikh would present a very long string of prayer beads to the sheikh, after having kissed the large bead which forms the head of the string. The sheikh would then place this string in front of the circle of participants. The string of beads was long enough for a large number of dervishes to be able to use it. Each of its beads was approximately the size of a human fist. Before beginning the* dhikr *each participant would kiss the segment of the string lying in front of him and grasp it in both of his hands.*

The sheikh would then recite slowly the following introductory formula: 'I take refuge in God from the evil of Satan'. Those in the circle would then begin the dhikr *[which was based on the word 'Allah'] by saying in unison the word 'Allah'.... As the* dhikr *progressed, the sheikh would begin to rotate the string of prayer beads counterclockwise around the circle. The* dhikr *would gradually speed up until the two syllables of the word 'Allah' become indistinguishable from each other and the bodies of the chanting dervishes began to sway frenziedly....*

The dhikr *was of indeterminate length. When the sheikh deemed the performance to have gone on long enough, he would slowly pronounce the word 'Allah', followed by the sentence, 'There is none greater than God; all praise be to God....' He would then say the following prayer: 'Bless this sacred time. May good be victorious. May evil be vanquished. May God fill us with his divine radiance and our hearts with the light of his name. May breath and peace be multiplied, the breath of Mawlana, the secret of Shams-ı Tebrizi, the beneficence of Imam 'Ali. Let us pronounce in unison,* Hu *[He, referring to God].' The dervishes would slowly pronounce the word [*Hu*], drawing out its sound until all the air had left their lungs. They would then, in unison, kiss the ground and rise to their feet. The sheikh would then walk among them, greeting them with the phrase, 'Peace be with you'.(12)*

The *sama'*, the whirling dance performed by the Mawlawis, should properly be regarded as a *dhikr*, because its purpose is the same as that of all *dhikrs*: to help the human spirit to ascend towards God. The onlooker may have regarded the *sama'* as nothing more than a pleasing performance, something akin to ballet. For the Mawlawi, however, this is not the case at all. For him it is a form of prayer, one which allows him to shut out the world entirely and draw near to God. It became a Mawlawi practice because Rumi himself was devoted to it. By drawing near to God through the *sama'*, Rumi gained the inspiration to write most of the *Mathnawi*. For this reason Bediuzzaman Firuzanfer has suggested that the *Mathnawi* should be regarded, not as a work of literature, but as a product of divine revelation.

For Mawlawis every detail of the *sama'* possesses a symbolic meaning. One example of this is the *muqabala*, the bow which each dervish accords to

The Major Tariqats

his fellows both before the whirling begins and after it ends. This bow symbolizes the respect which Mawlawis feel all men should have for each other. The way in which the dervishes hold their arms and hands during the *sama'* is symbolically important. The upturned palm of the raised right hand is open to the sky which symbolizes the dwelling place of God. The downturned palm of the left hand is directed toward the earth, the dwelling place of man. The dervish himself can be viewed as a conduit of grace from above which he channels to the world below.

The Koran states that all creation, consciously or unconsciously, is in a perpetual state of prayer and worship.

> *The seven heavens and the earth and all that is therein praise Him, and there is not a thing that does not hymn His praise.(13)*

The *sama'* is a form of conscious participation in this prayer and worship, for its whirling movement is the characteristic motion of the microcosm and the macrocosm, of everything which makes up the universe from atoms to the heavenly bodies.

The hauntingly beautiful music which accompanies the *sama'* possesses a symbolic dimension. The Mawlawis liken the plaintive sound of the reed flute, the instrument of key importance in this music, to the cries of the lonely and bewildered human soul yearning for God.

The Mawlawis, unlike the Bektashis, never departed from the teachings of their founder. This is perhaps due to the fact that Rumi's thoughts were set down in works of such great literary merit. These works are beloved not only by Mawlawis, but by all Turks.

Chapter Eleven

The Khalwatis

The dervish commonly regarded as the founder of the Khalwati *tariqat* is Abu 'Abdillah Siràjuddin 'Umar b. Akmaluddin al‑Lahji al-Khalwati (d. 750/1349 or 800/1397). He is said to have been born in Lahijan, which is located in the Gilan province of Iran. While still a youth, however, he went to Khwarizm where he became a student of his uncle, a sufi named Akhi Muhammad b. Nur Khalwati. After the death of this uncle (717/1317), 'Umar became the spiritual leader of his uncle's *murids*. He later moved to Azerbaijan and then to Egypt. He left Egypt and performed the *hajj*. He then went to Khorasan, where he settled in the city of Herat. There he established the *tariqat* which came to bear his name.

The title al-Khalwati was given to al-Lahji because he frequently secluded himself for contemplation. The Arabic word *khalwat* is used by sufis to mean "retirement for devotion or contemplation"; the form *khalwati* means "a practitioner of *khalwat*". According to a Khalwati tradition, al-Lahji was given the name al-Khalwati by worried disciples who discovered him after a prolonged search praying in the hollow of a plane tree.

'Umar was succeeded by Sayyid Yahya Shirwani (d.862/1429). During his tenure as sheikh the *tariqat* attracted a large number of adherents. Shirvani's assistants went forth from Khorasan to establish Khalwati *tekkes* in every part of the Muslim world. The *tariqat* enjoyed a period of extraordinary growth, especially in Anatolia and the Balkans. With the passage of time the *tariqat* split into four distinct groups: the Jamalis, the Ahmadis, the Ruşanis, and the Shamsis. The eponymous founders of these groups were: Jamal Khalwati, also known as Çelebi Khalifa (d. 899/1493 or 903/1497), Ahmad Shamsaddin Marmaravi (d.910/1504), Dede 'Umar Ruşani (d.935/1528), and Shamsaddin Ahmad Sivasi (d.1006/1597). In time each of these four groups split into numerous sub-groups. By the end of the nineteen century the Khalwati *tariqat* consisted of no less than fifty separate brotherhoods, each of which has often been regarded as a distinct *tariqat*. If, however, we consider that all of these brotherhoods hold a basic set of beliefs and ceremonies in common, it seems better to regard them all as members of one great unity: the Khalwati *tariqat*.

The Major Tariqats

This ramification is illustrated by the following chart which sets forth the descendants of the Shabani branch of the Jamalis.

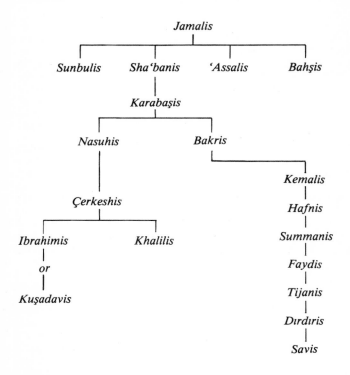

The Khalwati *tariqat* attracted various noteworthy Ottomans into its ranks. These included fifteen sultans, as well as the famous nineteenth-century historian, Jawdat Paşa (d.1825). This is not to imply, however, that it was a *tariqat* which appealed mostly to the educated elite. On the contrary, the Khalwati *tariqat* attracted people from a wide variety of backgrounds and social classes. According to a study made towards the end of the nineteenth century, the Khalwatis had more *tekkes* in Istanbul than any other *tariqat*. At that time Istanbul contained eighty-nine Khalwati *tekkes*, compared to twenty-two Nakshbandi *tekkes*, five Mawlawi *tekkes*, and three Shadhali *tekkes*. (1) In Turkey today, despite the official closure of all *tekkes* in 1925, the Shabani, Jarrahi and ʿUşşaqi groups are still active. The collective membership of these

Illustration 23

Illustration 24

94

Illustration 25

Illustration 26

Illustration 27   SCHEÏKH des MEWLÉWYS.

DERWISCH MEWLÉWY. *Illustration 28*

Illustration 29

Dervich
ou Moine Turc qui tourne par devotion

99

Illustration 30

three Khalwati groups is larger than that of any other *tariqat* active in Turkey today. The Khalwati *tariqat* is also the largest of the *tariqats* still active in the Balkan countries.(2)

The Khalwatis believe that a man in search of God must pass through seven successive stages before he can achieve his goal. A sheikh can recognize which stage a man is on by carefully observing his physical and spiritual state. A man who is in the first stage possesses a *nafs-i ammarah* (a nature that is a slave to fleshly desires). He is a man who is amoral; he is a prisoner of his basic instincts and passions. He who has reached the second stage is someone who, having become aware of the baseness of his desires, feels shame for those of his actions which he now recognizes as sinful; he is a man of conscience. For this reason he is said to possess a *nafs-i lawwamah* (a nature that is inclined to self-reproach). If he is sufficiently successful in freeing himself from the prison of his passions he will eventually reach the third stage, the stage of those who possess a *nafs-i mulhamah* (a nature that has been inspired by God). A man who has arrived at this stage endeavors to obey all God's commandments as revealed by the Koran and the *sunnat* of the Prophet (i.e. to live his life according to the *shari'at*). His resolution wavers, however, as he is still partly dominated by his passions. If he successfully masters all his passions, he acquires a *nafs-i mutmainnah* (a nature marked by assurance). As God has promised salvation to all those who faithfully obey His commandments, a person who has acquired this nature is at peace: he is a man of assurance because he is able to live his life in perfect conformity to the *shari'at*.

Once a man has become the possessor of a *nafs-i mutmainnah*, he is ready to enter the fifth stage, a stage in which he turns in a more intimate way toward God by turning away from the world as completely as possible. In this stage he is said to possess a *nafs-i radiyah* (a nature marked by willingness). A man in the fifth stage practices asceticism in order that he may make his soul completely willing to turn towards God. Once a man's soul has fully turned toward God, he can enter the sixth stage. In this stage he ceases to concentrate his energies on practicing asceticism. He returns to the world in order that he may serve his fellow men by leading them to God. A man in this stage is said to possess a *nafs-i mardiyah* (a nature with which God is content). From this stage a man may strive to pass to the seventh and final stage. A man who enters this stage becomes the possessor of a *nafs-i kamilah* (a perfect nature). In this stage a man has drawn so near to God that he is said to dwell in God. As God makes perfect all who dwell in Him, a man who has reached this stage is said to have a perfect nature.

It should be noted that a man who has become the possessor of a *nafs-i kamilah* is, despite his inner spiritual state, a man whose appearance and actions are outwardly unremarkable. By retaining this unremarkable appearance he is better able to accomplish the work to which he must now devote himself: the work of leading men to God. It is work which is best accomplished, not by overawing people, but by winning their trust and affection in an unobtrusive way.

The Major Tariqats

With each of these stages there is associated a name or group of words pertaining to God. These are collectively known as the *asma-i sab'a* (the seven names). They are as follows:

> Stage One : *La ilaha illallah* (There is no god but God)
> Stage Two : *Allah* (God)
> Stage Three : *Hu* (He)
> Stage Four : *Haqq* (The Truth)
> Stage Five : *Hayy* (The Living One)
> Stage Six : *Qayyum* (The Everlasting One)
> Stage Seven : *Qahhar* (The Overwhelming One)

The Khalwatis believe that the proper recollection and contemplation of each of these seven names can draw aside ten thousand of the seventy thousand veils of light and darkness which, according to a saying which sufis have attributed to the Prophet Muhammad, lie between God and man. Each of these seven names is thus the basis of a *dhikr*. The perfect performance of one of these *dhikrs* is sufficient to draw aside ten thousand of these veils. For this reason the perfect performance of all seven of these *dhikrs* is sufficient to dispel all of the seventy thousand veils. A man who has gained a *nafs-i kamilah* is thus someone for whom all of these veils have been parted. He is, in other words, someone who has seen God.

One ritual of initiation used by the Khalwatis is performed as follows: The candidate comes before the sheikh and kneels down in front of him. He seats himself cross-legged facing the *qiblah* and begins to meditate, striving to empty his consciousness of all thoughts save those that pertain to God. When this has happened he turns his head towards the left and pronounces the words *La ilaha* (There is no god). He then turns his head to the right and repeats emphatically the words *illallah* (but God). He chants the words *La ilaha illallah* in this way a minimum of thirty-three and a maximum of one hundred and sixty five times. He then performs a second *dhikr* based on the word *Allah*. The ritual then concludes with his performing *dhikrs* based on the words *Hu, Haqq, Hayy, Qayyum,* and *Qahhar*. It will be noted that these *dhikrs* collectively constitute the *asma-i sab'a*, mentioned above.

There is a *dhikr* which all the members of a *tekke* perform together. It is known as the *dawaran* (rotation). Before this *dhikr* begins all of the members of the *tekke* proceed in single file into the main room of the *tekke*. There they form a circle which includes their sheikh, who stands with his back to the *mihrab*. As soon as the sheikh begins to pronounce the words of the *dhikr*, all the dervishes place their arms upon the shoulders of those on either side of them. Thus linked, they begin to move in unison, first taking a few steps to the left and then taking a few steps to the right. While circling in this way they chant the words *Hu* and *Allah*. As the *dhikr* progresses, the movements of the dervishes become faster and more agitated; and their chantings become ecstatic.

Chapter Twelve

The Qadiris

The spread of the Khalwati *tariqat* within Anatolia and the Balkans has been matched by that of the Qadiri *tariqat* within the Islamic word as a whole. Its founder, 'Abd al-Qadir Gilani (d.561/1166) was an extraordinary man, respected even by Ibn Taymiyah, an Islamic theologian who was vehemently opposed to sufism.

Abd al-Qadir Gilani was born in 470/1077 in Gilan, an Iranian province situated on the south coast of the Caspian Sea. He died in Baghdad in 561/1156. Qadiris say that he was "born of love, lived in a perfect way, and died having achieved the perfection of love." If we interpret the phrase *kamal-i ashq* (perfection of love) according to *abjad*, a mystical interpretive system in which each letter of the Arabic alphabet is assigned a numerical value, we find that the sum of the numerical value of the letters in the word *kamal* (perfection) is 470, a figure which is the same as that of the Islamic lunar year in which Gilani was born. The word *ashq* (love) when interpreted according to this system, yields a sum of 91, a figure which equals Gilani's age at the time he died. The phrase *kamal-i ashq* (the perfection of love), when evaluated in this way, yields the number 561, the Islamic lunar year in which Gilani died. Qadiris believe that these mystical computations support the claim that Gilani was the possessor of *kamal-i ashq*.

When Gilani was eighteen years old he journeyed to Baghdad where he completed his education. He studied law under Qadi Abu Sa'id Mahrami, literature under Abu Zakariya, and the *hadith* under Bakr al‑Muzaffar.He was attracted, however, by sufism. For this reason he abandoned his studies and went to a lonely spot near Baghdad where he lived as a solitary ascetic for twenty-five years.

While he was living in this way he became a full-fledged dervish, joining a *tekke* in Baghdad headed by Abu Sa'id al-Mubarak. Gilani later became the head of his own *tekke*. Many of his adherents must have been initially attracted to him by his preaching. We are told that the crowds that came to hear him preach were so great that Gilani had to preach to them in the open, as no single building was large enough to accommodate them. We are fortunate that a number of his sermons have been preserved in a work entitled *al-Fath al-rabbani* (The Divine Conquest).

Perhaps the most remarkable of Gilani's attributes were his tolerance and his charity. T. W. Arnold says of Gilani that "in none of his books or precepts are to be found any expressions of ill will or enmity toward Christians." He then goes on to say that "whenever he *Gilani* spoke of the People of the Book, it was only to express his sorrow for their religious errors, and to pray that God might enlighten them. Arnold calls this tolerance "a striking characteristic of his followers in all ages".(1) H. A. R. Gibb echoed this when he wrote:

The Major Tariqats

The Qadiri order is on the whole amongst the most tolerant and progressive orders, not far removed from orthodoxy, distinguished by philanthropy, piety, and humility, and averse to fanaticism, whether religious or political.(2)

The Qadiri *tariqat* established by Gilani and his disciples was based in Baghdad. From there it spread throughout the Islamic world. Eşrefoğlu 'Abdullah Rumi (d.874/1469) was responsible for establishing it in Anatolia. This Turkish scholar and poet received his initial training in sufism from the Khalwatis and the Bayramis. He later joined a Qadiri *tekke* in Damascus. After he returned to Anatolia he devoted himself to expounding the Qadiri approach to God. (3) Another outstanding Turkish Qadiri was Ismail Rumi (d.1041/1631), who was instrumental in establishing the Qadiris in Istanbul. Ismail, like Eşrefoğlu, had originally been a Khalwati.

In more recent times, the Qadiris have been noted for their missionary activities in West Africa. For a description of these activities let us again turn to T. W. Arnold:

In the beginning of the nineteenth century the great spiritual revival that was so profoundly influencing the Muhammadan world, stirred up the Kadiriyye [i.e. the Qadiris] of the Sahara and the Western Sudan to renewed life and energy, and before long, learned theologians or small colonies of persons affiliated to the order were to be found scattered throughout the Western Sudan from the Senegal to the mouth of the Niger. The chief centers of their missionary organization are in Kanka, Timbo (Futah-Jallon) and Musardu (in the Mandingo country). These initiates formed centers of Islamic influence in the midst of a pagan population, among whom they received a welcome as public scribes, legists, writers of amulets and schoolmasters; gradually they would acquire influence over their new surroundings, and isolated cases of conversion would soon grow into little bands of converts, the most promising of whom would often be sent to complete their studies at the chief centers of the order, or even to the schools of Kairwan or Tripoli, or to the universities of Fez and al-Azhar in Cairo. Here they might remain for several years, until they had perfected their theological studies, and would then return to their native place, fully equipped for the work of spreading the faith among their fellow-countrymen. In this way a leaven has been introduced into the midst of fetish-worshippers and idolaters, which has gradually spread the faith of Islam surely and steadily, though by almost imperceptible degrees. Up to the middle of the nineteenth century most of the schools in the Sudan were founded and conducted by teachers trained under the auspices of the Kadiriyye and their organization provided for a regular and continuous system of propaganda among the heathen tribes. The missionary work of this order has been entirely of

The Qadiris

a peaceful character, and has relied wholly on personal example and precept, on the influence of the teacher over his pupils, and on the spread of education. In this way the Kadiriyye missionaries of the Sudan have shown themselves true to the principles of their founder and the universal tradition of their order.(4)

The Qadiri *tariqat* has a large number of adherents in the Muslim world today, especially in North Africa, Iraq, Turkey, and the Balkans. In Turkey the Qadiris are now most numerous in those provinces which lie along the coast of the Black Sea.

The following description of the Qadiri initiation ceremony is taken from a work entitled *Tibyan al-wasail* (The Explanation of the Means), by Haririzade Muhammad Kamaladdin:

> *After calling the* murid *before him, the sheikh recites the* fatihah *three times: He then says, 'Great God I ask your forgiveness'. After this he takes the right hand of the* murid *and recites the following confession:*
>
> *'I witness to the existence of God, the angels and the prophets. I repent of all my sins before God and take refuge in the Messenger of God. I will keep the commandments of God and the Prophet. I will refrain from doing what they have forbidden. I will, to the best of my ability, make it a practice to hasten to the aid of the helpless and the downtrodden. 'Abd al-Qadir Gilani is our guide in this world and the next. May God witness this our confession.' The* murid *then recites the same confession.*
>
> *The* murid *next kneels before the sheikh and closes his eyes. The sheikh then says: 'The hand of God is one with the hand of our sheikh and founder. It is 'Abd al-Qadir Gilani who is your example. The covenant is with God and the Prophet.' After this the sheikh, and then the* murid *, say, 'There is no god but God.' A tuft of hair is then cut from the* murid's *head to symbolize that he has now set himself apart from all but God. Following this the sheikh and the* murid, *along with all others who are present, turn toward the* qiblah *and say, 'God is most great.' The sheikh then recites a prayer.*
>
> *The ceremony ends with a reading of the* fatihah *in honor of the prophets and the saints who constitute the* silsilah *of the* tariqat.*(5)*

The Qadiris begin their common *dhikr* by reciting the first *surah* (chapter) of the Koran three times. This is followed by a recitation of the following verse taken from the second *surah* of the Koran:

> *"Allah! There is no god save Him, the Alive, the Eternal. Neither slumber nor sleep overtaketh Him. Unto Him belongeth whatsoever is in the heavens and whatsoever is in the earth. Who is he that intercedeth*

The Major Tariqats

with Him save by His leave? He knoweth that which is in front of them and that which is behind them, while they encompass nothing of His knowledge save what He wills. His throne includeth the heavens and the earth, and He is never weary of preserving them. He is the Sublime, the Tremendous.(6)

The *dhikr* then continues with the recitation of these Koranic verses, which are also taken from the second *surah*:

The messenger believeth in that which has been revealed unto him from His word and (so do) the believers. Each one believeth in Allah and His angels and His scriptures and His messengers—We make no distinction between any of His messengers—and they say: We hear, and we obey. (Grant us) Thy forgiveness, our Lord. Unto Thee is the journeying.

Allah tasketh not a soul beyond its scope. For it (is only) that which it hath earned, and against it (only) that which it hath deserved. Our Lord! Condemn us not if we forget, or miss the mark! Our Lord! Lay not on us such a burden as Thou didst lay on those before us! Our Lord! Impose not on us that which we have not the strength to bear! Pardon us, absolve us and have mercy on us, Thou, our Protector, and give us victory over the disbelieving folk.(7)

After reciting other Koranic verses the assembled dervishes perform a *dawaran* (rotation) ceremony which is very similar to the one performed by Khalwatis. The dervishes stand and form a circle. They place their arms over the shoulders of those next to them. After closing their eyes they begin to rock their heads first to the left and then to the right. As they do this they chant the Divine Name, *Hu* (He). The circle of dervishes begins revolving to a musical accompaniment. As the tempo of the music increases the circle revolves more rapidly. Gradually the movements, chanting, and music cause the participants to become ecstatic. As the ceremony progresses the Divine Name, *Hu*, is replaced first by the Divine Name *Allah*, and then by the words *La ilaha illallah* (There is no god but God). The volume of the chanting increases as the participants become progressively more agitated. In past times it was common to observe dervishes overcome by ecstasy collapsing, or casting themselves to the ground, during the ceremony. The ceremony ends with recitations of the *fatihah*, verbal salutations to the Prophet, and a prayer.

Chapter Thirteen

The Nakshbandis

The Nakshbandi *tariqat* was founded by Bahaaddin Muhammad b. Muhammad al-Bukhari (d.791/1388). He was born near the central Asian city of Bukhara in 710/1318. Tradition has it that when Bahaaddin was three days old the sufi sage Muhammad Baba Sammasi visited his village. It was there divinely revealed to Muhammad Baba that Bahaaddin was destined to become one of the greatest of God's servants. Upon learning this Muhammad Baba adopted Bahaaddin as his spiritual son and charged his assistant Sayyid Amir Kulal with the child's spiritual training. We know little about Bahaaddin's early years apart from the fact that he studied for a time in Samarqand and then moved to Nasaf, where he became a *murid* of Amir Kulal (d.777/1375). According to Bahaaddin's own testimony, however, the sufi sheikh who most influenced him was not Amir Kulal, but Abdulkhaliq Ghujduwani (d.617/1220), a sheikh who, though long dead, appeared to Bahaaddin in visions.

Abdulkhaliq Ghujduwani was one of the two most outstanding disciples of Yusuf Hamadhani (d.535/1140); the other was Ahmad Yesevi. Ghujduwani taught his disciples to approach God according to a method which became known as the *tariq-i khwajagan* (The Way of the Teachers). He is also supposed to have formulated eight principles which Bahaaddin later made a part of the Nakshbandi creed. These were as follows:

> *1)* hush der dem, *awareness of breathing,*
> *2)* nazar ber qadam, *watching over one's steps,*
> *3)* safar der watan, *internal mystical journey,*
> *4)* khalwat der anjuman, *solitude in the crowd,*
> *5)* yad kerd, *recollection,*
> *6)* baz gerd, *restraining one's thoughts,*
> *7)* nigah dasht, *to watch one's thought, and*
> *8)* yad dasht, *concentration upon God.(1)*

When Amir Kulal died in 1379 his disciples acknowledged Bahaaddin as their new *murshid*. This group of disciples was the nucleus of what was to become the Nakshbandi *tariqat*. The Nakshbandi way to God was first promulgated in Anatolia by a certain Molla Ilahi (d.896/1409), and it still commands followers in Turkey today.

The Nakshbandi initiation ceremony is not marked by complicated ritual. On the day of his initiation the *murid* first performs the ritual ablution known as the *abdast*. He then goes before his sheikh, seats himself opposite him, and kisses his hand. The sheikh places one of his hands on one of the *murid's* hands

The Major Tariqats

and says a prayer. He then recites the first *surah* of the Koran, the *fatihah*.

The sheikh then admonishes the *murid* to go through life with a smiling, cheerful countenance, as Nakshbandis believe that the face is the mirror of the soul. The sheikh advises him to be like the sun in his compassion, like the dust beneath the feet of his fellows in humility, like a corpse in his submission to all that may befall him (it is from God), like the night which shrouds the faults of others in darkness, and like a river which flows with generosity.(2) After imparting this advice to the *murid*, the sheikh gives him one thousand prayer beads with which he is to perform in private the *dhikrs* which the sheikh assigns to him. The *murid* is to perform these *dhikrs* until, as Nakshbandis would say, each breath and beat of his heart intones the assigned Names of God.

When a Nakshbandi performs his *dhikr* in private, he is instructed to keep the physical image of his *murshid's* face in his mind throughout the *dhikr*. He is asked to focus his attention on that part of the *murshid's* forehead which lies midway between his eyebrows, as this is held to be the point from which the *murshid's* divine inspiration emanates. This part of the *murshid's* face is, as it were, a gateway through which the *murid* passes as he journeys toward and returns from the ineffable presence of God.

This idea of *dhikr* is greatly informed by the belief that imitation of the *murshid* can lead the *murid* to God. Successful imitation of the *murshid* is dependent on the *murid's* ability to efface his own personality to the point where its outlines become lost in those of the personality of the *murshid*. Sufis view this process as analogous to the wondrous obliteration (*fana*) that takes place when a human soul comes face to face with God.

The most important of the *dhikrs* performed by the Nakshbandis is based on the word *Allah*. They also perform *dhikrs* based on various *surahs* of the Koran. Those who have been fully initiated into the *tariqat* can participate in a common *dhikr* known as the *Khatm-i khajagan* (Prayer of the Teachers). Before they begin this *dhikr* the dervishes seat themselves in a circle. The *dhikr* begins with the repetition of various expressions of repentance.These are followed by the repetition of other prayers. When these have been concluded the assembly repeats the sentence, "I ask for God's forgiveness," a specified number of times. They then repeat the sentence, "There is no god but God", the same number of times. After this they verbally salute the Prophet Muhammad and his family. This portion of the *dhikr* then concludes with the recitation of various chapters and verses of the Koran.

The rest of the *dhikr* is based upon a contemplation of death. The dervishes first ponder the transitory nature of life. They then imagine that they themselves have died. They contemplate their worldly goods being taken over by others. They envision their bodies being placed in coffins. Finally, they consider the time when they will be asked to account for their deeds in this world, keeping in mind the fact that only their good deeds will avail them in the next world. They then begin to chant the word *Allah*, the word which gives them hope when they contemplate death. This chant is followed by a reading of some portion of the Koran and a prayer said on behalf of the great Nakshbandi figures in the past. After this prayer has been offered the service is at an end.

Chapter Fourteen

The Rifaʻis

The Rifaʻi *tariqat* was one of the first *tariqats* to become established in Anatolia. Its founder was Ahmad Rifaʻi (d. 571/1175). He was born in Iraq of a family which claimed descent from the Prophet Muhammad. Like the Prophet, he was both orphaned at an early age and raised by one of his uncles. This uncle, Mansur al-Batayihi, was also to become his *murshid*.

Ahmad Rifaʻi had memorized the entire Koran by the time he was eight years old. As a young man he studied under two men who were well known for their knowledge of *hadith*, Sheikh Abul Fadl ʻAli al-Wasiti, and Abu Ghalib ʻAbdullah b. Mansur. He studied Islamic law with several leading Shafiʻi lawyers. His keen intellect in combination with his immense learning enabled him in later life to produce some twenty written works. Among those of his works which have come down to us the most famous are *al-Burhan al-muayyad* (The Confirmed Proof), and *al-Hikam* (The Wisdom). In his dealings with his fellow men he was noted for his compassion and his generosity towards those in need. One example of this was his practice of gathering firewood for impoverished widows and orphans.

Upon the death of his uncle, Mansur al-Battayihi, Ahmad Rifaʻi became the *murshid* of his uncle's disciples. As time passed others were attracted to this group. From it in time the Rifaʻi *tariqat* developed. It was a *tariqat* which had a large membership scattered throughout the Islamic world. In Ottoman times its *tekkes* were numerous in Anatolia and in the Balkans. It still has a considerable number of adherents in what is now the Republic of Turkey.

In the centuries which followed Ahmad Rifaʻi's death many practices which he would have condemned crept into the *tariqat*. The following passage, which is taken from an Englishman's observations of Egyptian life in the period 1825-1835, vividly depicts what a number of these practices were:

> *[Among] the most celebrated order of dervishes in Egypt are ...*
> *the Rifayyeh [i.e. The Rifaʻis].... Its banners, and the turbans of its*
> *members, are black; or the latter are of a very deep-blue woolen stuff,*
> *or muslin of a very dark greenish hue. The Rifaʻee dervishes are*
> *celebrated for the performance of many wonderful feats. The "Il-*
> *waneeyeh", or Owlad 'Ilwan, who are a sect of the Rifaʻees, pretend*
> *to thrust iron spikes into their eyes and bodies without sustaining any*
> *injuries; and in appearance they do this, in such a manner as to deceive*
> *any person who can believe it possible for a man to do such a thing in*
> *reality. They also break large masses of stone on their chests; eat live*
> *coals, glass, and are said to pass swords completely through their bodies,*
> *and packing-needles through both their cheeks, without suffering any*
> *pain, or leaving any wounds [the practice of penetrating both cheeks*

with skewers was common among dervishes of this order]; to hollow out
a piece of the trunk of a palm-tree, fill it with rags soaked with oil and
tar, then set fire to these contents, and carry the burning mass under
his arm, in a religious procession (wearing only drawers), the flames
curling over his bare chest, back and head, and apparently doing him
no injury. The "Saadeeyeh", an order founded by sheikh Saad-ed-Deen
El-Gibawee, are another and more celebrated sect of Rifa'ees.... Their
banners are green; and their turbans, of the same color or of the dark
hue of the Rifa'ees in general. There are many darweeshes of this order
who handle, with impunity, live venomous serpents, and scorpions....
On certain occasions (as for instance, on that of the festival of the birth
of the Prophet), the Sheikh of the Saadeeyeh rides, on horseback, over
the bodies of a number of his darweeshes, and other persons, who throw
themselves on the ground for the purpose; and all assert that they are
not injured by the tread of the horse....(1)

In his autobiography, one of Turkey's best known contemporary novelists
has recorded his childhood memories of a Rifa'i ceremony conducted in the
tekke to which his father belonged in Istanbul. He writes,

I too was among the chanters.... As we chanted we were caught
up in a wave of excitement. The atmosphere of contagion is difficult
to explain. Some ten dervishes continuously whirled in the middle of
the sama'hana *and I was whirling among them. One felt that flight was*
imminent, that one's feet were about to leave the ground. While ten or
so dervishes whirled, with billowing robes and skirts, a dozen others
were burying skewers in their cheeks... driving them through their mouths
until they protruded from the opposite cheek. With skewers pro-
truding thus from their cheeks they began to whirl and chant.
On all four sides of the sama'hana *there were wooden posts. Some*
among the remaining dervishes began using wooden mallets to drive the
skewers protruding from the cheeks of their brethren into these posts.
Two or three dervishes were nailed to each post. These dervishes con-
tinued their chanting without interruption. Other dervishes, kneeling on
sheepskins placed at intervals around the sama'hana, *were chanting "Ya*
Hay, ya Qayyum!... Ya Hay, ya Qayyum!..." in tempo with the sheikh
as they turned their heads first to the right and then to the left. After
some time they began to chant 'Allah, Allah!' in place of this original
chant.
When the excitement had reached its peak, the final and most
dramatic of the ceremonial displays commenced. Several swords were
produced, razor sharp, with narrow blades on which verses of the Koran
and poems had been engraved. A number of dervishes began to draw
the keen cutting edges of these swords across their tongues, after which

The Major Tariqats

they showed that the razoredged blades had not cut them. Then the sheikh arose and opened his robes to the waist. Two dervishes held a sword between them, one grasping the sword's hilt and the other the tip of its blade. The sheikh draped himself over the blade, his head hanging down on one side and his feet on the other... his whole weight supported by its cutting edge ....(2)

Sensational displays such as these became characteristic of the Rifaʻi *tariqat*, not just in Egypt and Istanbul, but throughout the Islamic world.

If, however, we examine those principles which constitute the fundamentals of Rifaʻi thought we see that beneath this sensational exterior there lay a core of sound belief. Yunus Ibrahim Samarrai has itemized these basics of the Rifaʻi creed as follows:

1) *Belief in the unity of God,*
2) *Acceptance of the Koran as the basis of religious obligation,*
3) *Devotion to the* sunnat *of the Prophet,*
4) *Continual performance of* dhikr *combined with continual self-searching,*
5) *Love,*
6) *Devotion to those beliefs held by the great men of Islam,*
7) *Respect for the companions of the Prophet,*
8) *Believing in destiny and in the fact that both good and evil come from God,*
9) *Contemplation of the universe as the work of God,*
10) *Praying with other Rifaʻis,*
11) *Behavior modeled on that of the Prophet,*
12) *Reading the Koran regularly and seeking to increase one's store of knowledge,*
13) *Avoidance of acts conducive to self-glorification and refusal to favor some people at the expense of others,*
14) *Avoidance of idle chatter, and*
15) *Rejection of all innovations which may be detrimental to the purity of Islamic faith and practice.(3)*

Kenan Rifaʻi (d.1950), one of the great modern sheikhs of this order, has left us the following description of the Rifaʻi initiation ceremony:

The murshid *[first] instructs the* murid *to purify himself by performing the Islamic ritual washing (*abdast*). This washing is regarded as an outward sign of the* murid's *repentance. The* murid *is then told to perform the Islamic ritual prayer two times. When this has been done the* murshid *turns toward the* qiblah, *kneels and sits back on his heels. The* murid *assumes this same position, but sits so that his knees are* *touching those of the* murshid. *The* murshid *then takes the* murid's *hands into his own and recites the first chapter of the Koran three times. He then recites this Koranic verse: 'Lo! those who swear allegiance unto thee (Muhammad) swear allegiance only unto Allah. The hand of Allah is above their hands. So whosoever breaketh his oath, breaketh it only to his soul's hurt while whosoever keepeth his covenant with Allah, on him will He bestow immense reward.'(XLVIII, 10) After this he recites various* hadith *which pertain to the swearing of oaths to God. The* murshid *then asks the* murid, *'Do you swear allegiance to me under these conditions?' After the* murid *has given an affirmative reply, the* murshid *asks God to pardon the* murid. *He then enjoins the* murid *to be loyal to the principles of faith and worship, to aid the poor and helpless, and to recognize no master save Ahmad Rifa'i. He declares that God and the Prophet are witnesses to this event. The ceremony concludes with prayers for all the great Muslims who have died, which number includes, of course, many venerable figures from the Rifa'i tariqat. These prayers are followed by a recital of the opening chapter of the Koran.(4)*

The first *dhikr* which the Rifa'i *murid* learns is one based on the sentence, "There is no god but God." The *murid* is advised to perform this *dhikr* alone in a place where he will not be distracted. Before he begins the *dhikr* he should seat himself so that he faces Mecca. He should then close his eyes and, invoking his sheikh's assistance, attempt to empty his mind and heart of all but God. Having done this he can begin the *dhikr*.

When the sheikh has decided that the *murid* has made sufficient spiritual progress, he asks him to start performing the *dhikr* based on the word *Allah*. As the *murid* increases in spiritual awareness the sheikh gives him various other words to be used as the bases of his *dhikrs*. These words are usually names of God. Those names which are most often used in *dhikrs* are: *Rahman* (The Merciful), *Rahim* (The Compassionate), *Wahhab* (The Giver), *Quddus* (The Host Holy), *Haqq* (The Truth), *Halim* (The Clement), *Hannan* (The Sympathetic), *Hayy* (The Living One), *Hafiz* (The Preserver), and *Hamid* (The One Who Is Worthy of Praise).(5)

All of the words mentioned above are also used in *dhikrs* which the members of a *tekke* perform as a group. Such *dhikrs* are preceded by the recitation of various prayers and Koranic verses. These *dhikrs* are often accompanied by music. The bizarre acts for which the Rifa'is have become well known were performed in the course of these common *dhikrs*. The *dhikrs* themselves are often chanted in such a loud and eccentric way that the Rifa'is have long been dubbed "The Howling Dervishes"

Chapter Fifteen

The Malamis

The name Malami is derived from the Arabic word *malamat* (reproach, blame, censure). In sufism *malamat* is always associated with *ikhlas* (sincerity, purity of heart), and *ikhlas* is in turn associated with making God the sole object of all one's thoughts, words, and actions.

Before becoming a sufi the normal condition of a man's heart is one of impurity or division. The heart is divided by many conflicting desires which, by pulling it in many directions at once, destroy its unity. As long as the heart remains in this condition the desire to approach God is at best one desire among many. By becoming a sufi one embarks upon a process by which the heart is gradually cleansed of all desires except the desire to approach God. In this way the purity and unity of the heart is restored. The general name for this process is *zuhd* (asceticism). *Malamat* is an advanced form of *zuhd* given special emphasis by Malamis.

Of the many objects of desire which contaminate the heart and dilute its desire to approach God, none is more alluring than the praise of other people. Sufis have always been keenly aware that people are social beings with a deep need to belong to, and be accepted by, a community. This need drives men to make conformity to the expectations of others one of their major concerns, and accounts in part for the deep satisfaction they take in the praise of others. Cleansing the heart of the desire for material possessions is relatively easy. Cleansing the heart of the desire for the positive regard of others is very difficult. Malamis believe that this can only be accomplished by cultivating the habit of self-reproach and, when necessary, behaving in a manner calculated to draw upon oneself the reproaches of others.

The Malami must learn to constantly ask himself such questions as, "Am I trying to maintain my reputation for piety, or am I trying to draw near to God?" In order to keep his heart pure, he must be engaged in a constant inspection of his motives. At the same time he must be prepared to destroy the positive regard others have for him, as it only feeds his innate desire to glorify himself. A striking example of this is contained in the story of a saintly dervish who was greeted with adulation by a large number of his admirers as he was about to enter a town. The dervish's response to this welcome was to stop and begin to urinate in full view of the crowd. The people became disgusted and left him saying that no such man could be a saint.(1) Sufis such as this dervish have often cited these two *hadith* in support of their views:

> *Allah doth not attend to your external appearance or material possessions, but to your hearts and actions.(2)*

> *My saints dwell under my auspices, and none but I may know them.(3)*

The Malamis

Historically, the best of the Malamis were saints indeed. They lived according to the *shari'at*, but they kept their piety concealed from public view. The worst of them, however, used the idea of *malamat* as a license to do exactly as they pleased. Most of those affiliated with the *tariqats* labeled *Malami* were neither saints nor charlatans, but sincerely religious people engaged in a struggle to know God.

Although sufis devoted to *malamat* have existed in all the *tariqats*, it is the followers of Hamdun al-Qassar, Haji Bayram, and Nur al-'Arab, whom the term Malami brings to mind. Although in later times *Malamis* who considered themselves followers of Hamdun al-Qassar (d.271/844) established themselves in Anatolia, the man who firmly implanted the Malami way in Anatolia was Haji Bayram (d.833/1429).

Haji Bayram, the founder of the Bayrami *tariqat*, began his career by teaching in a school in Ankara. While there he became so attracted by the sufi teachings of Hamiduddin Aksarayi, a dervish who lived in Kayseri, that he abandoned his teaching career to become a sufi. He became Aksarayi's closest disciple. When Aksarayi died, Haji Bayram was regarded as his spiritual successor. He founded the Bayrami *tariqat* in Ankara.

The Bayramis frequently found themselves in conflict with the Ottoman authorities, owing to their refusal to curry favor with those in power. The history of their *tariqat* is thus filled with incidents of the arrest, imprisonment, and execution of its leaders and many of their followers.

The Malamis in Turkey today belong to a *tariqat* founded by Sayyid Muhammad Nur al-'Arab, who is usually referred to as Sayyid Muhammad Nur. He began establishing what was to become the Nuri *tariqat* in Skoplije, in what is today Yugoslavia. The Bayramis were gradually absorbed into this new Malami *tariqat*.

Nur al-'Arab was born in Egypt of a family which was descended from the Prophet Muhammad. He became a *murid* of Sheikh Hasan al–Kuwayni, a teacher at the al-Azhar madrassa in Cairo. After studying at al-Azhar, Nur al-'Arab travelled extensively in the Islamic world. During this period he became associated with the Nakshbandi, Khalwati, and Akbari *tariqats* respectively. He eventually went to Skoplije where he became a teacher in a madrassa. A number of people there, including the Ottoman governor, Servili Salim Paşa, found Nur al-'Arab's ideas on sufism attractive. These people were to become the nucleus of his *tariqat*.

The Nuri *tariqat* which he founded is unusual in that it possesses no *tekkes* and its members wear no distinctive clothing. Nuris also reject all supererogatory religious practices, as such practices are a temptation to self-praise, and also cause those who engage in them to become the object of public praise. Nuris, like all sufis, strive to draw near to God; what makes them distinctive is that they strive to make their striving as inconspicuous as possible.

Although the Nuris perform conventional *dhikrs* based on the names of God or on Koranic verses, they also regard conversation with their *murshids*

115

The Major Tariqats

as being in itself a form of *dhikr*. They in fact view it as the most important kind of *dhikr*.

Illustration 31

KHALWETY.

DERWISCH NIYAZY. Illustration 32

OEUS CHAKY.

Illustration 34

Illustration 35

SCHEÏKH des CADRYS.

DERWISCH CADRY

Illustration 36

Illustration 37

SCHEÏKH des RUFAYIS.

124

DERWISCH RUFAYI

Illustration 38

Postscript

As we conclude this brief view of Turkish sufism it seems fitting to mention Kuşadalı Ibrahim (1188/1774-1262/1845), a Khalwati sheikh who espoused a view which has relevance for sufis in Turkey today. Kuşadali felt that the ceremonies, distinctive clothing, and buildings of the *tariqats* were not at all in accordance with the true spirit of sufism, which always emphasized inner purity over outward display. For this reason he proposed, in essence, that sufis jettison these things and begin once more to practice the kind of sufism that existed before the *tekkes* came into being. He seems to have envisioned a situation in which a *murshid* who lived, not as a sheikh in a *tekke*, but as an ordinary person in the workaday world, might slowly enlighten a handful of *murids* who would then go forth to enlighten others. Such sufis would certainly be Malami in that they would be inconspicuous in their virtue.

It is to be hoped that Kuşadalı's ideas will eventually gain the wide attention they so greatly deserve.

Illustrations

Topkapı Sarayı Müzesi (TSM) = Topkapı Palace Museum
Divan Edebiyatı Müzesi (Dv.E.M.) = Diwan Literature Museum

1. Mendicant Dervishes. *Preziosi*, **Stambul: moeurs et costumes,** *ed. Canson (Paris, 1883),* *T.S.M., Y.B. 2669, pl.2.*

2. Whirling (Mawlawi) Dervishes. The whirling dance of the Mawlawis is a form of mute *dhikr*. Its movements are said to imitate those of the universe itself. The upturned palms of the dervishes' right hands are open to the sky, which symbolizes the dwelling place of God. The palms of their left hands are turned down toward the earth, which symbolizes the dwelling place of man. As they dance the dervishes become a channel through which grace from above flows into the world below. **Ibid.,** *p.20.*

3. A Young Mawlawi Dervish. In sufi poetry the rose is often a symbol for worldly love. Worldly love, like the rose, possesses an ephemeral beauty. As all worldly things are fated to pass away, so that love which makes these things its object must also pass away. Sufis believe that worldly love yearns to become divine love. Divine love is love which has made God its object. As God alone is everlasting, so is divine love. *Mid- eighteenth-century Ottoman miniature, Album no. H.2155, fol.39 r., T.S.M. .*

4. A Muslim Performing the *Salat. Salat* is the first of the four pillars of Islam. It is an exercise of devotion which all Muslims are required to perform five times a day. Sufis have always sought to perform the *salat* more frequently than either the Koran or the *hadith* enjoin them to do. All Muslims are expected to perform the *salat* at dawn, at midday, in the afternoon, in the evening, and at sunset. Sufis, however, have long made it a practice to perform a *salat* in the middle of the night, a practice referred to as *tahajjud. Mouradgea d'ohsson,* **Tableau general de l'empire ottoman,** *(Paris, 1987), T.S.M., Y.B. 3441, Vol. 1, pl.14.*

5. A Muslim Performing the *Abdast* (ritual ablution). A Muslim can perform the *salat* only after he has cleansed himself by performing the *abdast*. Sufis have discerned mystical meanings in all the religious rituals prescribed by the Koran. In the head movements a Muslim must make while performing the *abdast* the sufi sage Ibn al-'Arabi saw the movements of a sinful man hanging his head in shame before God. He interpreted this to mean that man needs to cleanse his heart as well as his body in order to truly worship God. *Ibid., pl.12.*

6. A Muslim at Prayer. **Recueil de cent estampes representant differentes nation du Levant, gravees sur les tableaux peints d'apres nature en 1707-1708 sur les ordres de M. de Feridl ambassadeur du roi a la Porte** *(Paris, 1714), T.S.M., Y.B. 1155.*

7. A Qalandari Traveler. This dervish is the representative of a marginal *tariqat* tradition with a presence in Anatolia dating back to the eleventh century. The more conservative adherents of this tradition were sufis whose beliefs and practices resembled those of the Malamatis (see Chapt. Twelve). There also existed Qalandaris of more extreme

school who practiced an exaggerated form of *malamat*. They shaved their hair, beards, and eyebrows. They eschewed all forms of conventional piety and provoked the criticism of others by intentionally flouting the accepted standards of dress and behavior. They did so in order that they might devote themselves solely to God. *d'Ohsson*, **op.cit.**, *pl.137.*

8. A dervish. This miniature may have been inspired by images of the extreme school of Qalandaris mentioned above. *Mid-eighteenth-century Ottoman miniature, T.S.M., Album no. H.2155, fol.28 v.*

9. A Roving Dervish. *Early seventeenth-century Safawid miniature, T.S.M., Album no. H.2155, fol. 37 v.)*

10. A Mawlawi *Tekke*. This eighteenth century gravure depicts the entrance to a Mawlawi *tekke* located in the Beyoğlu district of Istanbul. The buildings which comprise the *tekke* complex presently house the Divan Edebiyatı Müzesi (Diwan Literature Museum). Dv. E. M., No. 332/1.

11. Roving Dervishes. *Seventeenth-century Safawid miniature, T.S.M., Album no. H.2155, fol. 33 r.*

12. *Chila*. A European's depiction of two dervishes undergoing *chila* (the forty day period of contemplative suffering required of those who wished to become initiates into sufi fraternities). *Chila* was both a means of testing the character of would-be initiates and also a spiritual exercise designed to cleanse their hearts of worldly concerns. Lying down during *chila* was deemed a sign of disrespect toward God. *d'Ohsson*, **op.cit.**, *pl. 134.*

13. Whirling Dervishes. This nineteenth-century painting by A. Bayot depicts Mawlawi dervishes whirling in the *sama'hana* of the Mawlawi *tekke* which now houses the Diwan Literature Museum. *Dv. E.M., No. 361.*

14. Genealogical Trees (*silsilahs*) of the Different Orders of Dervishes. Sufi *murids* came to place great emphasis on the spiritual genealogies of their *murshids*. *Murids* came to regard as legitimate only those *murshids* who could trace their spiritual genealogies back to the Prophet himself. **Ibid.**, *pl. 102.*

15. A Dervish Blowing a *Nefir* (horn). The *nefir* is an ins.   .ment associated with the Bektashis. It may have been originally used by Turkish tribesmen for sounding the charge in battles or giving alarms. Its close association with the Bektashis may be due to their having adopted it for ceremonial purposes. *Early eighteenth- century miniature by the Ottoman artist Levni, T.S.M., H.2164, fol.22 v.*

16. A Babai Dervish. *d'Ohsson*, **op.cit.**, *pl.116.*

17. A Bektashi Dervish. This gravure illustrates the emphasis the *tariqats* came to place

Illustrations

on symbolic clothing. The dervish is wearing the Bektashi *taj* (a hat consisting of twelve segments, which symbolize the Bektashi allegiance to the Twelve Imams), a *khırka* (dervish cloak), and a *kamar* (belt) to which a stone with twelve fluted edges (misrepresented by the artist) called a *teslim taşı* (stone of surrender) is attached. He wears three such stones around his neck to signify the Bektashis' belief that Muhammad, 'Ali, and Allah are all united in one godhead. A *nefir* (see illustration 15) is inserted in his belt along with a backscratcher. He holds a begging bowl suspended by a thin chain in his right hand (the artist was probably unaware of the fact that the Bektashi *tariqat* frowned on begging more than did most other *tariqats*). Dervish begging bowls were usually made from either coconut shells or ebony and were often engraved with Koranic verses and floral motifs. The dervishes of almost every *tariqat* habitually carried a string of prayer beads which they used when they performed *dhikrs*. This Bektashi dervish is holding a double- headed *teber* (axe). Although the Bektashis had once used the *teber* as a weapon, by the late Ottoman period it had become merely a relic of their martial past, one which they used to ornament the walls of their *tekkes*. **Ibid.**, *pl.114*.

18. A Bektashi Sheikh. **Ibid.**, *pl.113*.

19. A Bektashi Traveler. **Ibid.**, *pl.115*.

20-21 Sheikh Baba's Battle With Some Brigands Who Are Attacking Sarı Saltuk's *Tekke*. *Miniature from an eighteenth-century manuscript of Fadıl Andaruni's* **Khamsa-i Atai,** *T.S.M., R.816, fol.78 v.*

22. Bektashi Emin Baba. The figure in the upper left is a nineteenth- century artist's depiction of a Bektashi *baba*. *Jean Brindesi,* **Elbise-i Atika: Musée des Anciens Costumes Turcs de Constantinople,** *(nineteenth-century), T.S.M., Y.B. 2672, pl.16.*

23. Mawlana Meeting Shams-i Tabrizi. *Miniature from an early seventeenth-century manuscript of* **Jami al-Siyar,** *T.S.M., H.1230, fol. 121 r.*

24. With the passage of time the *tariqats* began to embellish the memory of the founders with stories of their miraculous deeds. This miniature (probably of the Baghdad school), illustrates one such story told of Mawlana according to which a cow which had escaped from a slaughterhouse bowed to the ground on sight of him. *Miniature from a late sixteenth-century manuscript of Abd al-Wahab b. Muhammad al-Hamadhani's* **Sawa-qib al-Manaqib,** *T.S.M., R.1479, fol. 171 r.*

25. Mawlana Conversing With a Sea-Monster. **Ibid.**, *fol. 171 r.*

26. Lala Mustafa Paşa's Visit To the Tomb of Mawlana. *Miniature from a late sixteenth-century manuscript of Gelibolu Mustafa Ali's* **Nusratnama,** *T.S.M., H.1365, fol. 36 r.*

27. A Mawlawi Sheikh. *d'Ohsson,* **op.cit.,** *pl.109.*

Illustrations

28. A Mawlawi Dervish. **Ibid.**, *pl.110.*

29. A Whirling Dervish (for reference see illustration 6 above).

30. A Whirling Dervish. **The Costumes of Turkey Illustrated By a Series of Engravings; With Descriptions In English and French,** *(London, 1802), T.S.M., Y.B. 3406, pl.46.*

31. A Khalwati Dervish. *d'Ohsson,* **op.cit.,** *pl.115.*

32. A Niyazi Dervish. The Niyazis were one of the many branches of the Khalwati tariqat. **Ibid.,** *pl.123.*

33. A Sunbuli Dervish. The Sunbulis made up another of the many branches of the Khalwati *tariqat.* **Ibid.,** *pl. 118.*

34. A Uşşaqi Dervish. The Uşşaqis are branch of the Khalwatis still active in Turkey today. **Ibid.,** *pl.122.*

35. A Qadiri Sheikh. **Ibid.,** *pl.106.*

36. A Qadiri Dervish. **Ibid.,** *pl.106.*

37. A Rifa'i Sheikh. **Ibid.,** *pl.107.*

38. A Rifa'i Dervish. **Ibid.,** *pl.108.*

39. A Mawlawi Dervish Seated On a *Post* (sheepskin) Playing a *Kudum* (drum). The *kudum* was used in the mystical music of the *tariqats* for establishing the tempo of the music played during communal *dhikr* ceremonies. *Kudums* used in mystical music are of two types: the Mawlawi *kudum* and the Rifa'i *kudum. Nineteenth-century water color painting, D.E.M. No. 366.*

40. A Mawlawi *Sama.* The *ney* (reed flute) and the *kudum* (drum) are an inseparable part of the Mawlawi's *dhikr,* known as the *sama. d'Ohsson,* **op.cit.,** *pl.133.*

41. The *Dawaran* (rotation) of the Qadiris. **Ibid.,** *pl.127.*

42-46 Illustrations Depicting Five Different Stages Of a Rifa'i *Dhikr. d'Ohsson,* **op.cit.,** *pls.128- 132.*

Notes

PART ONE

1. The Koran and Sufism

1. **Kor.** VI:103-105.
2. See **Kor.** XXIV:35.
3. **Kor.** V:54.
4. **Kor.** XXXI:33.
5. **Kor.** III:14.
6. **Kor.** XXIX:64.
7. **Kor.** LVII:20.
8. **Kor.** XIII:28.
9. **Kor.** XVII:78-9; see also **Kor.** III:17; LI:16-18; LII:48-9; LXXIII:6-8.
10. **Kor.** XXIX:2-3.
11. See Alexis Carrel, **L'Homme, cet inconnu**, (Buenos Aires, 1945), p.103.
12. **Kor.** XXIV:35-42.

2. The *Sunnat* and Sufism

1. **Kor.** XXXIII:21.
2. Muhammad Hamidullah, **Initiation à l'Islam**, (Paris, 1970), p.204.
3. Abu Nu'aym al-Isfahani, **Hilyat al-awliya**, III, 231.
4. Ibn Sa'd, **al-Tabaqat al-kubra**, (Beirut, 1960-65), III, 394-95.
5. Abu Nu'aym, 1, 80.
6. Abul Qasim 'Abdulkarim al-Qushayrı, **al-risalah**, (Cairo, 1962), Intro., pp.8-9.
7. **Ibid.**, pp.8-9.
8. Abu Talib Makki, **Qut al-qulub**, (Egypt, 1961), 1, 244.
9. Yaşar Nuri Öztürk, **Hallac-ı Mansur ve Eseri**, (Istanbul, 1976), p.65.
10. 'Ali al-Qari, **Sharh al-shifa**, (Istanbul, 1307), 1, 503; Isma'il b. Muhammad 'Ajluni, **Kashf al-khufa**, (Beirut, 1351), 1, 265.
11. Abu 'Isa Muhammad al-Tirmidhi, **al-Sunan**, *manaqib*, 1.
12. Abu 'Abdillah Muhammad al-Bukhari, **al-Sahih, manaqib**, 23.
13. Öztürk, **op.cit.**, p.65.
14. al-Qari, I/508; 'Ajluni, II/127.
15. **Ibid.**, 2/163.
16. **Kor.** XXXIII:21.
17. Ibn Hisham, **al-Sirat al-nabawiyah**, (Egypt, 1375), I,501-2.
18. Ibn Sa'd, I, 23.
19. al-Bukhari, *anbiya'*, 48.
20. Sulayman al-Sijistani Abu Da'wud, **al-Sunan**, *taharat*, 4.
21. Ibn Sa'd, II, 194.
22. al-Bukhari, *faraid*, 15.

Notes

23. **Kor.** V:82-85.

3. The *Murshid* and *Zuhd*

1. **Kor.** III:31.
2. **Kor.** XLVIII:10.
3. N.T., **John** 3:3.
4. **Kor.** XXIX:20.
5. Ajluni, II, 402.
6. Ahmad Faruqi Rabbani, **Maktubat**, *maktub I*, p.165.
7. Yaşar Nuri Öztürk, **Hazret-i Fatima**, (Istanbul, 1983), p.153.
8. 'Abdulwahhab Sha'rani, **Lawaqih al-anwar**, Egypt, 1299. *tabaqat*, I, 39.
9. Ibn Abi'l-Khayr Abu Said, **Asrar al-tawhid fi maqamat al-shaykh Abi Sa'id**, (Egypt, 1966), p.360.
10. Rif'at Ahmad, **Mir'at al-maqasid**, (Istanbul, 1293), p.195.
11. Ajluni, I, 203.
12. **Ibid.**
13. The Age of those who were personally acquainted with the Prophet. The Age of the Companions is said to have come to an official close upon the death of Amir b. Wasil al-Kinani Abu'l-Tufayl in 100 A.H., styled the last of the Companions.
14. The classical sufi conceptions of *fana* and *baka* were first formulated by al-Karraz (d.286/899).

4. The Rise of the *Tekke*

1. Kuşadalı is using the word *ghaza*, which normally means "holy war", to signify "life lived in accordance with all God's commandments as revealed in the Koran and by the *sunnat* of the Prophet."
2. Yaşar Nuri Öztürk, **Kuşadalı Ibrahim Halveti**, (Istanbul, 1982), p.89.
3. Abdurrahman Jami, **Nafahat al-uns**, tr. Lami'i, (Istanbul, 1270), p.86.
4. See Fuad Köprülü, **Türk Edebiyatında İlk Mutasavvıflar**, (Ankara, 1984), p.196; Annemarie Schimmel, **Mystical Dimensions of Islam**, (Chapel Hill, 1975), pp.231 ff.
5. See Schimmel, **ibid.**, pp.203 ff.
6. See **Kor.** III:200; VIII:6.
7. See Ibn Manzur, **Lisan al-'arab**, art. on *rabt*; **Qamus**, art. on *rabt*.
8. See Fuad Köprülü, art. on *ribat*, *"Vakıflar Dergisi"*, No. 2, 1942, pp.267-69.
9. Abu Nu'aym, *hilyah*, IX, 386.

5. Three Great Sufi Thinkers

1. Schimmel, **op.cit.**, p.57.
2. Abu Nu'aym, *hilyah*, X, 255
3. **Ibid.**, X, 255.
4. The English translation is taken from A. J. Arberry's **Sufism, An Account of the Mystics of Islam**, (London, 1942), p.80.

Notes

5. The English translation is taken from Iqnaz Goldziher, **Introduction to Islamic Theology and Law**,tr. Andras and Ruth Hamori, (Princeton, 1981), p.152.

6. The *Tariqats*

1. See Ibn Manzur, art. on *tariq*.
2. See **Kor.** XX:63, 104; LXXII:11,16.
3. See Sayyid al-Sharif Jurjani, **al-Ta'rifat** (alphabetical), art. on *tariq*.
4. See Schimmel, **op.cit.**, pp.239 ff.
5. For examples of the missionary role played by the *tariqats*, see T.W. Arnold, **The Preaching of Islam**, (London, 1913).
6. Zaki Mubarak, **al-Tasawwuf al-islami**, I, 42.
7. Dhahabi, **Tadhkirah**, (Beirut, 1956), I, 67.
8. See Isma'il Haqqi Bursavi, **Sharh-i usul-i 'asharah**, (Istanbul, n.d.), pp.38-44.
9. See Shamsaddin Muhammad Nuri, **Risala-i muraqabah**, (Istanbul, 1282), pp.12-20.
10. See Yaşar Nuri Öztürk, **Kuran ve Sünnete Göre Tasavvuf**. (Istanbul, 1979), pp.130-150.

PART TWO

7. The Yesevis

1. See Köprülü, **op.cit.**, p.41.
2. See **Nafahat**, art. on Abu Al Farmadi.
3. Kemal Eraslan, **Divan-ı Hikmetten Seçmeler**, (Ankara, 1983), p.55.
4. **Ibid.**, p.63.
5. **Ibid.**, p.67.
6. **Ibid.**, p.89.
7. **Ibid.**, p.89.
8. **Ibid.**, p.101.
9. **Ibid.**, p.105-9.
10. **Ibid.**, p.113.
11. **Ibid.**, p.121.
12. **Ibid.**, pp.133-35.
13. **Ibid.**, pp.169-171.
14. **Ibid.**, p.191.
15. **Ibid.**, p.293.
16. **Ibid.**, pp.50-51.
17. **Ibid.**, pp.51-52.
18. **Ibid.**, p.52.
19. Köprülü, **op.cit.**, p.105.

Notes

8. *Futuwwat* and the *Akhis*

1. See Shihabuddin Abu Hafs 'Umar Suhrawardi, **'Awarif al-ma'arif**. (Egypt, 1968) chapt.30; Ibn al-'Arabi, **op.cit.**, 2/232 ff.
2. **Kor.** LIX:9.
3. **Kor.**IX:111.
4. See Ibn al-'Arabi, **op.cit.**, 2/233 ff.
5. See **Ibid.**, 2/233 ff.
6. See Claude Cahen, **Pre-Ottoman Turkey**, tr. J. Jones-Williams, (New York, 1968), p.196.
7. Neşet Çağatay, **Bir Türk Kurumu Olan Akhilik**, (Konya, 1981), p.95.
8. Ibn Battutah, **Tuhfat al-Nuzzar**, tr. Mehmet Şerif, (Istanbul, 1335), 1/310-346.
9. Yılmaz Öztuna, **Büyük Türkiye Tarihi**, (Istanbul, 1977-79), II, 50.

9. The Bektashis

1. Esad Coşan, **Haji Bektaş-i Walinin Maqalatı**, (Ankara, n.d.), p.3.
2. **Ibid.**, XXXVII.
3. **Ibid.**, p.48.
4. **Ibid.**, p.35.
5. **Ibid.**, p.71.
6. **Ibid.**, p.35.
7. **Ibid.**, pp.14-16.
8. **Ibid.**, p.102.
9. **Ibid.**, p.19.
10. **Ibid.**, p.80.
11. **Ibid.**, pp.62-64.
12. **Sharh-i basmalah**, ed. Rüştü Şardağ, (İzmir, 1985), p.94.
13. **Ibid.**, p.110.
14. **Ibid.**, p.106.
15. Coşan, **op.cit.**, p.108-109.
16. See Ibn Sa'd, **op.cit.**, 2/200-203.
17. Aziz Mahmud Hudai, **Waqi'at**, Süleymaniye (Esad Efendi) Library, No.1792-1793, I, 19v.
18. Murat Sertoğlu, **Yunus Emre, Hayatı ve Divanı**, (Istanbul, n.d.), pp.35-36.
19. **Ibid.**, p.61.
20. **Ibid.**, p.84.
21. **Ibid.**, p.93.
22. **Ibid.**, p.170.
23. **Ibid.**, p.189.
24. **Ibid.**, p.221-222.
25. **Wilayatname-i Haji Bektaş** (Gölpınarlı manuscript) p.90-91.
26. F.V. Hasluk, **Christianity and Islam Under the Sultans**, (Oxford, 1929), II, p.565.
27. See Ahmad Rifat, **Mir'atu'l-maqasid**, (Istanbul, 1293), pp.185 ff.
28. This word is frequently used by sufis as a benediction.
29. John Kingsley Birge, **The Bektashi Order of Dervishes**, (Hartford, 1937), p.175.

Notes

30. Enver Behnan Şapolyo, **Mezhepler ve Tarikatlar Tarihi**, (Istanbul, 1964), pp.284-85.
31. Birge, **op.cit.**, p.20.
32. There are an estimated three million Bektashis living in Turkey today. These Bektashis compose part of a larger population of Turks called Alawis. Historically, the Alawis have been distinguished from their Sunni neighbors by their belief in the Twelve Imams and the doctrine that 'Ali was the true successor of the Prophet. Some Alawi groups, such as the Kızılbaş and the Tahtacıs, adopted Bektashi beliefs and practices. Although groups such as these have not infrequently been called Bektashis, and although they have often identified themselves as such, Bektashis themselves have reserved the term only for those whom they regard as fully initiated members of recognized Bektashi *tekkes*.

10. The Mawlawis

1. The word Rumi, which we shall use when referring to Mawlana Jalaluddin, means "of Rum".
2. Abdülbaki Gölpınarlı, **Mevlana Celaleddin**, (Istanbul, 1985), pp.69-71.
3. **Ibid.**, p.130.
4. Gölpınarlı, **Mesnevi, Tercemesi ve Şerhi**, (Istanbul, 1983), I-II cilt, p.14.
5. Abdülbaki Gölpınarlı, **Rübailer**, (Istanbul, 1964), Quatrain 112.
6. Gölpınarlı, **Mesnevi Tercemesi ve Şerhi**, p.111.
7. **Ibid.**, p.30.
8. **Ibid.**, p.183.
9. **Ibid.**, p.113.
10. Gölpınarlı, **Mesnevi, Tercemesi ve Şerhi**, (Istanbul, 1983), III-IV, p.273.
11. This is the only part of the ceremony which is known to be based on a practice devised by Rumi himself.
12. Gölpınarlı, **Mevlana'dan Sonra Mevlevilik**, p.411.
13. **Kor.** XVII:44.

11. The Khalwatis

1. See Ahmad Münib Bandırmalızade, **Majmu'a-i takaya**.
2. Owing to the efforts of the late Muzaffer Ozak (d.1985) who was a Jarrahi sheikh in Istanbul, the Khalwati *tariqat* gained a number of European and North American adherents.

12. The Qadiris

1. T.W. Arnold, **The Preaching of Islam**, (London, 1913), p.325.
2. Hamilton Gibb, **Mohammedanism: An Historical Survey**, (London, 1949), pp.155-56
3. Sadiq Wijdani, **Qadiriyah**, (Istanbul, 1338-1340), pp.48 ff.
4. Arnold, **op.cit.**, pp.328-29.
5. Muhammad Kamaladdin Haririzade, **Tibyanu wasail al-haqaiq fi bayani salasil al-taraiq**, Süleymaniye (İbrahim Efendi) Library, I, 9-10.
6. **Kor.** II:255.
7. **Kor.** II:285-86.

13. The Nakshbandis

1. Schimmel, **op.cit.**, p.364.
2. Enver Behnan Şapolyo, **Mezhepler ve Tarikatlar Tarihi**, (Istanbul, 1964), p.145.

14. The Rifa'is

1. E. W. Lane, **The Manners and Customs of the Modern Egyptians**, (London, 1908), pp.248-49.
2. Aziz Nesin, **Böyle Gelmiş Böyle Gitmez**, (Ankara, 1972), pp.65-67.
3. Yunus İbrahim, **al-Sayyid Ahmad al-Rifa'i**, (Baghdad, 1970), passim.
4. Kenan Rifai, **Ahmad al-Rifa'i**, (Istanbul, 1340), pp.155 ff.
5. Mustafa Tahralı, **Ahmad al-Rifa'i, sa vie, sa oeuvre et tarique**, (doctoral dissertation, Paris, 1973), pp.372-79.

15. The Malamis

1. Schimmel, **op.cit.**, p.86.
2. Muslim, *birr*, 33; Ibn Maja, *zuhd*, 9, 60.
3. Ruzbihan Abu Muhammad Baqli, **Mashrab al-arwah**, ed. Nazif Hoja, (Istanbul, 1973), p.294.

Index

Index

Index

138

Index

Illustration 39

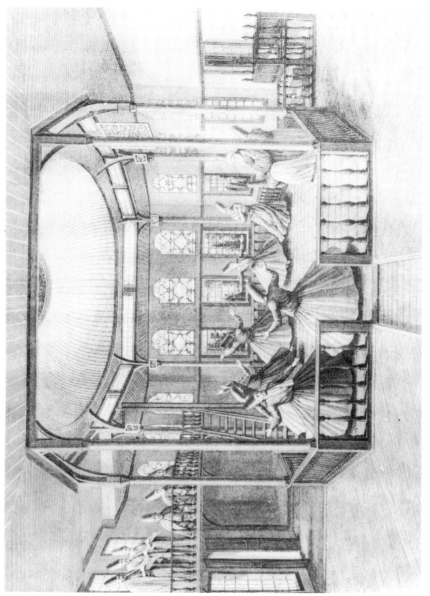

DANSE DES DERWISCHS MEWLÉWIS.

Illustration 40

DANSE DES DERWISCHS CAIROS

Illustration 41

143

EXERCICES DES RECRUES PRUSSIENS.

Illustration 42

EXERCICES DES DERWISCHS RUFANIS
II. SCÈNE.

Illustration 43

Illustration 44

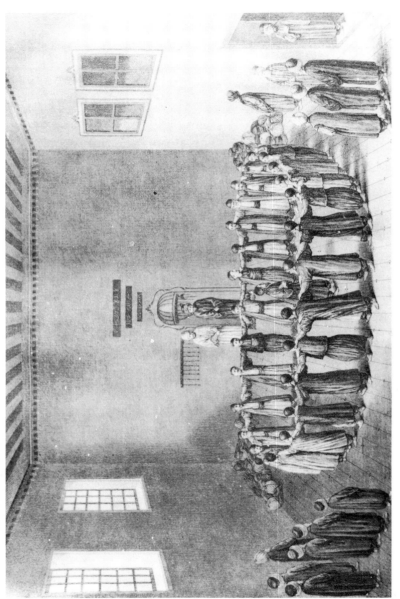

EXERCICES DES DERWISCHS RUFENTS
H.ASFAI

Illustration 45

147

Illustration 46